MUTUAL FUNDS

*A Comprehensive Guide
to Diversify your Investments*

TABLE OF CONTENTS

Introduction

"Investing puts money to work.
The only reason to save money is to invest it."

Grant Cardone

If you are reading this book, you probably got tired of all the stress and pressure you put yourself through at work for all your life. Can you imagine studying for more than 20 years only to work for 40 years more? That, my friend, is my definition of chains and lack of freedom. What kind of life have you built then? Sure, you get a degree, learn more from the workplace, improve for a chance of promotion. For what? To wake up at 4:00 in the morning, make breakfast, tidy up and organize yourself, go to work, get stressed at work, deal with a bunch of insensitive people, and go home, feeling tired, only to repeat the cycle over and over again for the rest of your life?

See, I am not persuading you into quitting your job nor am I dissuading you from getting one. But think about what you are earning as a regular person earning minimum wage. You pay for your lunch and transportation. You pay for your bills and your children's tuition. You consider having insurance to make sure your family gets enough when things do not go right. For over ten, twenty years of service, what have you earned by then?

Soon, you will be on your 50's and 60's, prone to various diseases such as diabetes, cancer, cardiovascular, and respiratory diseases. What will you do by then? How will you fend for yourself and your family's needs? For me, a stable way of spending my last years of living would be enjoying every bit of time left for me. I would travel the world, try new things, and accomplish my bucket list. Being in a day-to-day job will not make your dreams come true for you. When you see some of your workmates who have it all figured out, they did not get their wealth from work. If you dig a little deeper, you will see that their job is just a way of passing time and getting an allowance. On the outside, they have their own businesses where they get the *real* money from.

If you are tired of all the routines, then you got the right book. Why do you want to invest money in the first place? Isn't it that you want to buy yourselves all the time in the world without getting to work? You want to build a place for your family to grow and develop without worrying about their needs and wants in life. You want to provide security for yourself and your family knowing that there are unstable and uncontrollable factors in this world that can compromise your health and safety.

Imagine this, once you have established a stable investment, its growth will be impenetrable. You can literally leave it behind and let your money multiply. Having this book with you is not a sign of weakness, as some people call investment a lazy man's work. Although a part of it is true because once you succeed, you can do whatever you want without worrying about any requirements, assignments, and work stress. However, the hardest part of starting an investment is the startup. In that phase, your vital force will be challenged by unspeakable means of life torture. So, if people think of you as a crazy person for having this book, I want you to challenge their arguments by proving them wrong. You can start by having a little bit of self-education, then you can work from there.

"Formal education will make you a living;
self-education will make you a fortune."

Jim Rohn

If you do not believe Jim Rohn, one of the best American entrepreneurs, read this book and venture towards a successful investment. But your research must not end here. You know what they say, "Experience is the best teacher." It is no use owning this book if you will not commit anyway. Yes, it is true what critics say, business is a risky journey. But what isn't, really? You risk your life every day. You make mistakes on a daily basis. But the reason why we keep moving forward is the expectancy of a reward coming our way if we persevere. We do not stop trying just because we experienced a setback or a difficult circumstance. If you want to continue on the road to a successful investment, you need to commit to fight and be strong despite all odds. Keep trying your best to succeed. Never let your failures stop you from persevering. Instead, let it be a beacon to lead you on a better path and learn from the shortcomings you encountered.

Give Yourself a Push

Investing in mutual funds does not only put you towards financial stability. But it can also help a person develop holistically. Shocking is it not? Here are the values that you need to develop as you go along your milestones towards success.

Determination

This refers to your sense of purpose, your drive, and your attitude towards your life. As you go along the path towards a successful investment, you will soon develop a sense of fortitude and grit. It is the process of establishing your mind into moving forward despite any challenge that life can bring. See, when the world tries to pull you down, and it will, you will need all the strength you have to persevere against these odds. Having the right amount of determination will make you bolder in making risky decisions. It gives you the assurance of resilience. No matter what comes, you know it in yourself that you can survive. And that my friend, is an essential value on the road to investment.

Integrity

A lot of people might wonder about the relationship of integrity to success in investment. Simply put, integrity refers to somebody's honesty of work, credibility, and trustworthiness. Nothing good ever happens by accomplishing goals through deceitful and treacherous means. Even though we see some people who have become successful by being straight-up dishonest, rest assured, their wealth will never last and their happiness will not be achieved. Think about the Law of Effect. Every behavior has its own consequence. You may not feel it in a short while. But in the long run, you will realize how important it is to watch out for your actions. Much like the concept of Karma, if you believe in it; whether the action is good or bad, there is always a counteraction.

In the road to a successful business, there will always be trials that can compromise your attitude. But I want you to remember to keep on doing the right thing. Even when others might not do the same or even when there is no other way out but to cheat, there is always a choice to make. You just have to believe in the good despite the badness in this world. I know it sounds prophetic or holy but doing the right thing, no matter how difficult it may be, really pays off in the long run. All you need to do is keep a clear conscience in all of your actions, and you're good to go. No shadows to haunt your happiness. No setbacks to bring you down on your way to a successful business venture.

Willpower

This value refers to your mental discipline. Your ability to discern and ward off temptations and any enticements that can distract you from your goals. It is true what they say, "Money is the root of all evil." When things are getting good, trials will become inevitable.

Whether it is gambling, smoking, drinking, and using drugs. I want you to help yourself create a stable mindset against these temptations.

The most dangerous phrase you should avoid is, "Just a little bit." That small nicotine, the small amount of joint, and alcohol is enough to derail you from thinking straight. Do not make the same mistakes as some investors do. With their voices, they are unable to think critically, solve problems, and decide censoriously. Eventually, they get so blinded by temporary happiness, and they eventually let their goals slip out of their hands.

Critical-Mindedness

People think that investing is a lazy man's job. Well, as you move forward towards your milestones, you will realize how difficult it is to discern a good decision from a bad one. Which is why, as you learn from your mistakes, you start to develop critical-thinking which is an essential tool for analyzing, decision-making, and problem-solving. But do not be dissuaded if you feel dumb or when you feel like you are not enough. Critical-thinking is not developed overnight. Even the smartest people gathered their critical-thinking skills from committing their own set of mistakes. As long as you are willing to reflect on your faults and wrongs, you will develop an unstoppable sense of critical thinking that will allow you to continually seek information, apply learnings, and predict the outcomes of your decisions.

Open-Mindedness

There is no such thing as one-way to people who venture in business. It will always be a trial-and-error. On the road to successful investing, you need to commit to being open to suggestions and learnings. Get as much data and education you need from experience. Force yourself to try even when it means committing a mistake. Because these are essential in building a system of information that can come in handy anytime you face a problem. That said, instead of avoiding the nails on the floor, pick them up so they cannot hurt you anymore. Much like in business, you need to open your mind to all possibilities. Who knows? That experience could be your big break!

Inquisitiveness

There will always be people who are more knowledgeable than you. As an aspiring businessman, I want you to be like a child who is open to knowledge. Stay curious even when you have learned so much. Because trust me, what you know is not even close to a quarter of what business has to offer. Based on their experiences, each expert has his own set of hacks he is willing to share to the world. Acknowledge each of them and never hesitate to ask questions. In doing so, you will be able to discover new things applicable to your goal. You can set your own standards that you can use to establish your target. Like we discussed earlier, business is a trial-and-error method. You never know what fits you the most until you have tried them all.

Chapter 1

Investment Vehicles

"When you invest, you are buying a day
that you don't have to work."

Aya Laraya

One of the most common investment vehicles used worldwide is the mutual fund. But first of all, what do we mean when we say investment vehicle? This is a product used by investors to generate profit or positive returns. It could be in the form of certificates of deposit, bonds, stocks, and exchange-traded funds. Simply put, it is their source of capital to start a business or invest to grow their money. There are many types of investment vehicles, namely:

Ownership Investments

From the name itself, a proprietor will delve into ownership of a particular asset in hopes to increase his profit using the said asset. An example of this is owning stocks or shares from a company. These represent a person's part ownership to a corporation's assets and earnings.

Lending Investments

Another type of vehicle called the lending investments focuses their money to be used by another person or entity in hopes that its return will generate profit or interest. Cooperatives are the most common users of lending investments. People invest their money for lending purposes with the expectancy to grow in value as time passes by. This is also common among banks who use Certificates of Deposit that locks money in a saving's account to generate a high-interest rate in a specific period of time.

Cash Equivalents

These are highly-liquid assets used in treasury bills, short-term government bonds, and other money market instruments. It is one of the most vital indicators of a healthy financial system. It reflects the ability of a company to pay their dues on a specific period of time. Cash equivalents are common among large companies. When they use treasury bills, it means they are lending the government money in hopes to generate profit in the long run. Short-term government bonds are much like treasury bills. Except for this time, the government lends to small investors as a form of financial security. The bonds are payable with periodic interest until its value is repaid on the indicated maturity date.

Pooled Investment Vehicles

When a group of investors collects their money to invest in an investment vehicle, then it is called a pooled investment. An example of this is the mutual fund. This type of investment vehicle is operated by an assigned manager to allocate the funds collected in hopes to generate profit. Much like being a stockholder, owners of the mutual fund share the risk and the profits. A mutual fund investment is likened as a starter pack for a company. It is a way to generate funds used as capital to invest in other investment vehicles.

Mutual Funds

Most people who are unaware of mutual funds believe that it is a waste of time and money. Little do they know how big it is as an opportunity. There are four facets of mutual funds: the investor, the fund manager, and the trustee's monitor.

The investors are the people who give out their money to the mutual fund. This is where you belong as a start-up investor. The fund manager, preferably from Asset Management Companies (AMC), is likened to be an engineer or a doctor of mutual funds. From the name itself, he is responsible for managing your mutual funds and diversifying it into the market. To make sure that the assets maintain their value and grow profits, we have trustees who monitor the money in the market. The trustees also ensure the efficiency of the fund managers in putting the money into the market.

Starting a mutual fund is actually easier than other forms of investment vehicles. Because you have a manager to make sure your money generates interest. All you need to do is set a goal, and go from there. But we will discuss more of this later. Mutual funds are a form of investment where you literally sleep while you earn. You can leave it all to your fund manager and wait for ten years or so to become a millionaire. You heard that right! Depending on your investment, you can earn as much as millions. Of course, the bigger the investment, the bigger the income.

Now, why do you need to wait for ten years or so? Well, there are factors that influence the money market industry like the economy and inflation rate. Sometimes, calamities and other unexpected factors can also contribute to the rise and fall of the interest rate in the money market. If you look at the picture below, you can see the upward trend of the graph. Think of it as your money in the market. If you withdraw your funds in the first quarter of a ten-year plan, you will generate less income from your investment. Depending on the current interest rate, you might even incur a loss.

Which is why it is important to keep investing until you finish your desired plan. But what if I want to continue investing more money even after the ten-year plan? Then, you can choose not to withdraw your funds and go for more years of investing to generate a larger income. I am sure that there are options in the market for you so your investment will not be as heavy and you will have more room for your needs and miscellaneous expenses.

Investing in a mutual fund is like saving money. But unlike the typical way of saving, in mutual funds, your money actually generates income while it revolves in the market. If your goal is a safe and secure retirement, then you can be a millionaire by the time you turn 60 years old.

Mutual funds also offer short-term investments. For example, you want to earn for your future house and lot, car, and college tuition for your kids. There are plans that will offer you short-term investments to make ready for your upcoming milestones. Amazing, isn't it?

But before you invest in anything. You need to ensure the quality and reliability of your fund managers. You need to learn how to discriminate a bad investment from a good one. Times these days are full of scams. So, before you choose, do prior research on the company, bank, or corporation.

Commonly-Used Terms

"Risk comes from not knowing what you are doing."

Warren Buffet

Before we move forward to other topics in investment, let me give you a quick tour on the commonly-used terms in investment. Needless to say, some of us are not well-equipped with knowledge about business jargons. So, to clarify some terms we will be using in the future, here are ten commonly-used terms in business:

1. Assets. These are the properties of a person or business that has value. This refers to the inventories, money, equipment, furniture, fixtures, and other products used to generate income.

2. Liabilities. These are your debts and loans incurred to maintain operations. It refers to your financial obligation to pay bank loans, credit card debts, and monetary debts to vendors.

3. Profit and Loss. This refers to your financial performance. It could be presented quarterly, annually, or semi-annually. A business entity acquires profit when there is a financial gain at the end of the business period. But if you lost money at the

end of the financial period, you have incurred a loss. This usually happens when an entity spends more than it can gain.

4. Expenses. These are the costs you pay such as bills, salaries, advertising costs, and other expenditures.

5. Cash Flow. This refers to the movement of money in and out of your business including income and expenses.

6. Capital. This is the total amount of money invested in a business. The capital is the blood of the business used for various expenses needed to gain profit.

7. Depreciation. We usually hear this term with regards to cars, buildings, and other equipment. Depreciation is the reduction of value as time goes by. Which is why used cars are sold for a smaller price compared to a brand new one. It is because of the wear and tear concept of equipment, machines, and structures. But there is one thing that does not depreciate – land. Sometimes, it even increases in value depending on the nature of factors playing around the transaction. For example, in the 1900s a particular land costs about $10,000. As time goes by and the value of money appreciates, then so does the value of the land. And for instance, if its location has become a tourist spot, then the value of the land can increase more because of its demand.

8. Valuation. This is usually conducted by prospective buyers or investors where they evaluate the worthiness of a business or an asset. A valuation is conducted to assess whether a business is worth investing for, or if an asset is worth buying.

9. Financial Report. The decision-making and strategies conducted by the entity are shown in the financial report. This includes the cash flow and expenses paid by the business.

10. Income Statement. This refers to the overall performance of an entity. It shows whether it has incurred a profit or loss.

Benefits of Investing in Mutual Funds

There are hundreds of myths about mutual funds. Some say that you need to be an expert to start in mutual funds. Others claim that you need a lot of money and experience before you start investing. But all of these are just tales to dissuade people because of the risk. Everything in life is risky. So, if we go down that road, we might as well make the most of it.

1. Smaller Capital. Unlike other investments, mutual funds do not require much capital. There are plans suited for your monthly income that will not compromise your regular expenses.

2. Lower Risk. Your pooled investment is not concentrated on single security of investment vehicle. Your fund manager will diversify your investment to many different securities to reduce the probability of incurring a loss. Even if one of those investment vehicles incur a low rate for return, you always have collateral to gain higher profit.

3. Lower Maintenance. We have to admit; we are not experts on the stock market or the whole money market. With the help of our fund managers, there is no need for us to gain the skills in stock investment. All we need to do is generate capital so our fund managers can diversify it to various vehicles.

4. Variety of Investment Vehicles. There are about 50 to 200 kinds of securities in the money market. It is up to the strategic planning of your fund managers where and when to invest your pooled money.

5. Discipline in Investing. There are many factors that make an investor too fearful or too greedy in investing. This can take a toll on his financial status in the money market. Mutual funds allow disciplined investing because you generate a plan with your fund manager to follow throughout the process. Your fund managers could be your financial adviser. They tell you what you should do and they guide your actions in terms of cash flow. They reduce your fear of trying and they dissuade you from being too greedy in making your investments.

Disadvantages of Mutual Funds

I do not want to imply that mutual funds are an easy way to a good life. Some people believe that once you have established a good start in the system, you are set for life. But that is not entirely true. There are factors that affect the growth of your investment. Which is why we need to be responsible even if we have fund managers. Here are the disadvantages of mutual funds that you need to watch out for.

1. An expense ratio refers to the cost that investors pay to maintain a mutual fund in the money market. The expense ratio encompasses all the managing fees and operating expenses needed to maintain a mutual fund balance. However, if an investor is unaware of the expense ratio, it could get out of hand and it may aid to the incurrence of loss. Usually, an expense ratio should be around 0.5% to 0.75%. An expense ratio greater than 1.5% is too much. The expenses paid vary from one fund to another. Experts show that a smaller fund generates more expense because of limited funding for covering operational costs. Which is why it is essential to get to know the expense ratio for your investment before you push through.

2. Abuse of power. There are instances when our fund managers become rogue and abuse their power over our

money. Some managers become too greedy to invest in securities that could compromise the hope of generating an income. Although there are trustees, some fund managers are cunning. There are instances when a fund manager bribes the trustees to look past their decisions. When things are uncontrolled, you might be incurring losses at the end of your business period.

3. Uncontrolled Taxes. As discussed earlier, there are inevitable factors that can affect the health of the economy such as a calamity. In this case, the interest rates may go up or down depending on the issued taxes on the economy. Although fund managers cannot do anything about this as well, it is in their best interest to make sure your money still generates profit rather than a loss. For example, there is an impending decline of interest in the stock market. Your fund manager might decide to pull it back from the stock market and invest it on treasury bills or bonds. In that way, your money will still generate income.

Chapter 2

Start-up for Mutual Funds

"Successful Investing takes time, discipline, and patience. No matter how great the talent or effort, some things just take time: You can't produce a baby in one month by getting nine women pregnant."

Warren Buffet

B efore we start off with investing in mutual funds, let us dig a little deeper about some the concept of mutual funding. There are two main kinds of mutual funds, namely: the NO-LOAD FUNDS and the LOAD FUNDS. First of all, a mutual fund loan is the expense incurred for the purchase or acquisition of a mutual fund investment. The cost from purchasing fund shares is called **front-end loads** while the loads from the acquisition of a mutual fund share are called **back-end loads**. These investments that require payments are referred to as the Load Funds. Those who do not require an investor to pay any of these expenses are called No-Load Funds.

So, what are their differences? Load Funds are used when a person wants to hire a financial advisor. But for those who know enough and want to do things on their own, they prefer the No-Load Funds.

Load Funds are bought for a reason. For starters, a financial advisor is vital to have a guide on the twists and turns of mutual investment. In purchasing No-Load Funds, you can save money from hiring an advisor. If you think you are skilled enough to handle matters on your own, you would settle for No-Load Funds. In the usual sense, No-Load Funds have a lower expense ratio compared to Load Funds. The costs incurred in the transaction come from the profit or return on investment from the original fund.

Once you have chosen which kind of funding to use in your investment, let us take a look at your prospective mutual fund share type. There are literally hundreds of classes of investment in a mutual fund. Since it is likened to be a basket-full of apples, it is difficult to choose what fits for your preferences without a thorough guide.

1. Class A Share Funds. These kinds of investment incur a front-end load. Meaning, you will be paying an advisor or a professional to help you through your goals. Usually, the amount paid for this transaction is 5% of your total funding. So, if you invest $20,000 of Class A Share Funds, you will have to pay $1000 as an expense. The total investment you will be putting in the market is $19,000 instead of $20,000. This investment scale is recommended usually for businessmen who can invest large amounts into the market in hopes to generate a higher return on investment.

2. Class B Share Funds. These funds carry a back-end load. Meaning, an investor will be purchasing a mutual shares fund and assigns a financial advisor to help him get through the process. This is the most common class in purchasing mutual funds. It is recommended among people who are starting up. Unlike Class A, this kind of investment does not require a lot of funds from the pocket. Sure, it could generate less income

because of the lower resources but it is enough to start off with mutual fund investment.

3. Class C Shares are like the Class A shares, except for its duration. Class A shares are good for a long period of time. But if you want a short-term investment, purchase Class C Fund Shares where you can withdraw your capital along with your profit as early as 3 years, depending on the plan. This is effective among investors who aim to start a business or buy a real estate in a span of 3 years.

4. Class D Shares are likened to be like the A, B, and C shares except it is a No-Load Fund. Meaning, you do not get a financial advisor. You do it all by yourself.

5. Advisor Shares. Also known as Class Adv Share Funds, these are no-load investments that usually has a .50% expense ratio. From the name itself, you will be working with a financial advisor to help you in your endeavors. If you are looking to start up, this could be a good option to ward off the extra expenses.

6. Institutional Class Funds, also known as "Inst," Class I, X, and Y. These funds are available to those who own an institution or those who are planning to build an institution. Usually, the minimum investment is $25,000 divisible to your partners and pool your resources to obtain a specific goal. The advantage of this investment is its low expense ratio and low risk. Since you will be choosing your partners, in this case, you will be assured of their credibility. Plus, you can assist each other in the process and tasks you need to accomplish in lieu of your major plans.

7. The R Share is a typical choice to those who aim to plan for their retirement. Hence, the letter R. Although there is no

load on this investment, the expense ratio is quite high and it may range from .25 percent to .50 percent.

8. Index Funds are a type of investment that aims to match a benchmark of a market index. A market index is referred to as the performance or rates in the stock market. The index fund is a do-it-yourself investment with the goal of obtaining profits using a low-cost investment vehicle. Although some index funds are recorded to have a load, it is highly unrecommended. The reason why people use index funds is the low-cost concept. Purchasing an index fund with a load negates the whole point of saving money from various investment expenses.

Before you start investing, it is essential to assess your needs and your goals. Setting your goals for the future will allow you to determine the right investment strategy for you. This is the time when you search for a financial advisor to help you with an investment blueprint. Remember to check the mutual funds available in the market before you open your investment account.

Earning Money for Funds

Before you start a mutual fund investment, it is important to have enough cash to start with. In this segment, I will be giving you tips on how to save more money on the road to a successful business venture.

Get a Job

This could be one of the most practical ways to earn money but it takes time, especially for others who have a low-paying job. To pass the time and earn as much as you can, look for a job with a salary that meets your financial obligations. Think of the amount you pay for the bills, food, children's tuition fee, clothes, and other necessities. As much as possible, look for a job where you can pay all of these dues and at the same time, earn money for investment.

Get a Raise

During the course of your career, ask for a job enrichment or a job enlargement, something that promotes you to a higher paygrade. However, this is not easy at all. You need to prove your worth to your company before you get promoted. There are seminars and conventions you need to attend. There may be lots of exams you need to accomplish. But if you are lucky enough, proving your bosses how deserving you are for a raise can do the trick. Just do your best and earn as much as you can.

Find Extra Work

There are people out there who want to earn so much that they look for other part-time jobs apart from their regular work. Some work at an office during the day and wait in bars at night just to gain extra money. However, this shifting could be a lot of work and it can take a toll on your physical well-being. If you want to try some online platforms where you can earn extra bucks, you can do so. There are various part-time online jobs out there ready to hire people.

Buy and Sell

You can also try to engage in buy and sell. From the name itself, you buy things from people and resell them at a higher price for profits. A lot of people engage in buy and sell for second-hand cars, cellphones, accessories, clothes and other goods. Just a quick tip when you engage in buy and sell, always make sure to assess the trends every now and then. Fads change and preferences vary over time. You need to be cunning in choosing the products to sell, or else, you will end up losing more money than gaining.

Money Saving Skills

This is the part where you really need to gain some control over your impulsive buying. Learn to discriminate between your needs and wants. As much as possible, if you can hold your money for your savings, it is highly recommended. When you get tempted to buy something off the internet, wait for one to two weeks to decide. In that span of time, you will start to realize that you have no use for it. This averts the issue of being too extravagant in shopping. If you have linked your bank accounts or credit card to shopping platforms, disconnect from them at once. This is to help you ward off any temptation of buying things you do not really need.

Another tip to help you with this goal is to have some friends and family help you. You can make them help you save money for your investment. If they like, maybe they will want to be in it too.

Loans

There are credit companies that allow citizens to loan money for their needs. To purchase a mutual fund, you can get a loan from a company with a low-interest rate so you can get started on your investment. Make sure to inquire about their plans and methods so you do not get any unwanted surprises from these loan agents.

The Fund Adviser

From my experience, the best advisors help in three ways: encourage you to look at the problem or opportunity from multiple angles; help you balance the tug of the short-term with important long-term priorities; and ask the tough questions you need to know to reach the best solution.

Margo Georgiadis

There is so much to learn from our teachers. No matter how intelligent or wise a person is, there will always be room for learning and improvement. On the road to a successful investment, it is essential to have a financial advisor to guide your every move concerning your cash flow. From the title itself, a fund advisor is someone who recommends actions to an investor. They give advice to investors on how to manage their wealth, how to deal with losses, and how to diversify their assets and gain more return on investment. You might get confused about the difference between a fund manager and a fund advisor. To settle things straight, a fund manager pools the investments of various individuals and diversify it into the market in hopes of generating income. On the other hand, a fund advisor merely suggests potential plans and activities to an investor with the goal of maximizing profits and minimizing risks. Both of these parties gain a potential amount of incentive from your investment. Hence, the existence of Loads Funds discussed in the previous chapter.

There are many advantages to having a mutual fund advisor. For start-up investors, having somebody who suggests what you need to do is very important to avoid idle time. They encourage you to take rational steps towards a good investment. Whenever you feel fear or anxiety about your venture, your financial advisor will assure you that there is nothing to be afraid of. Fund advisors do not merely share their opinions on how you should manage your wealth. Rather, they base their advice on their own research and experiences in their years in the financial industry.

Your financial advisor will help you get in control of your emotions and impulses. He makes sure you never go beyond or below the boundary of fear and greed. Your advisor helps you think and walk straight on the path of investment and he can help ward off any temptation that can derail you from your goals.

Another advantage of having a fund manager is the ability to relax. Whenever people do not have an advisor, they usually stress themselves from thinking too much about their own financial blueprint. But with an advisor, he can help you brainstorm and concoct a viable plan to better your investment. You can assess your needs and shortcomings reliably and solve it using competent strategies. No matter how much people think that having a financial advisor is useless, I choose to believe otherwise. Having a fund advisor can do wonders for your investment. You just need to find the right one. But what should you look for in a fund advisor? Looking through a bunch of portfolios can be a difficult thing to do especially when you have no criteria to use in judging.

Let us start off by having someone who can be trusted – somebody who makes his decisions firmly and never leads his client down a road full of deceit. On the road to a successful investment, it could be helpful to join summits, conventions, and seminars in hopes to learn more about the venture. But this can also assist you in looking for a reliable fund advisor. He might be someone who is highly recommended by other business experts, someone who is said to have various successful experiences in guiding investors to prestige. Talk with some people in the summit and try to share your future plans of investment. Who knows? The person you are talking to might be your potential advisor.

Once you have listed the names of possible fund advisors, do your research about each and every one of them. Check their profiles and experiences. What do their former clients say about them? What kind of investments do they assert themselves in particular? Also, remember to check their records for disciplinary actions. You would not want to have somebody who had a history of deceitfully advising their clients. Check their verification as a certified financial advisor in the Financial Industry Regulatory Authority or FINRA's website.

They must have a Series 6 or 7 license or a 66, 65, and 63 Series License.

It is also vital to choose somebody who is paid out of a successful investment. This is to make sure that they perform at their peak whilst being an advisor. When a person is paid even when he does not meet any criteria, then he has no reason to push through his limits and work harder. A financial advisor must be the same. To some people, this might seem unfair. But for your own safety and security in the investment venture, you will need someone who is in it for success like you are. Be sure you speak the same language literally and figuratively. Your financial advisor must understand your goals and make sure everything falls into place in lieu of your dreams.

During your one-on-one interview with a potential financial advisor, there are various questions you can ask to break the ice. You can start by asking him about his investment projections. How does he see an investment? How does he usually run financial investments? And what are his usual strategies to maximize profit and minimize risk? You can make him explain simple and complex concepts that you cannot understand well. The way he explains and the way you understand each other is a vital factor to see whether or not you can work together as a team.

Lastly, before you sign any contract, read the papers and fully understand them. Examine and be speculative of each clause. Do not be afraid to seek counsel or ask questions if you do not understand. Watch out for any statement that says that there is a possibility for you to have speculative investments. By signing this clause, your right to report and pursue arbitration for mismanagement and deceit is revoked.

Chapter 3

The Search for a Fund Manager

As discussed in the previous chapter, some managers may abuse their power over your money and use it greedily in the market. Which is why in this segment, we will be tackling how to choose a reliable and competent fund manager. When you search the internet alone, hundreds of companies will persuade you to choose their service. Of course, in the beginning, they appear to be very consistent and experts in their line of work. But once they get a hold of your money, who is to say they will not scam you afterward? A fund manager is like an engineer. You tell him your plans for the future and he generates a blueprint to build the best building suited for you. In mutual funds, the manager is responsible for strategizing your money in the market to target your goals for the short-term or the long-term.

Imagine if you hired an engineer who lacks integrity. All he wants is the salary. Even if you give him the exact amount to buy the standard materials for the building, he chooses to purchase substandard resources to build your home. Imagine using substandard cement, paint, bearings, and iron in construction. Your newly-built edifice will be killing your budget for maintenance. Apart from that, calamities can easily destroy the roofing and structure of your home, making it unsafe to live in.

That is what happens when you choose the wrong fund manager. Set your standards high and be keen to details. Because therein relies on the success of your investment. In choosing a manager, here are tips to consider:

1. Tied Heart Towards Success. One of the most important factors to consider in looking for a fund manager is his dedication to his work – his passion and his drive to really help his clients to have what they deserve. Of course, you cannot assess one's love for work through meeting him in a day. You need a thorough investigation of his work, performance, and reviews. Tell him about your problems. Share your goals and your aspirations. Ask the obvious questions. From there, you can see how patient and remarkable his personality is. Trust your mind where it leads you in talking with fund managers. Be as inquisitive and curious as you can to see whether or not they are reliable in their line of work.

2. Dedication to Focus and Perform. Choose a fund manager whose budget is tied to his performance. There are others who get paid whether or not they become successful in their money management. As a clever move, choose a fund manager who will do anything to generate his income. Choose someone who is sure to perform at his finest to get his own incentives.

3. Consistent and Remarkable Results. Dig up the files of your prospective fund managers and focus on their strategy. One good tip to look for in a fund manager is the consistency of their methods with remarkable results. In the money market, there are temptations that will push a fund manager to change his line of strategy. Most of the time, these changes of tactic cause loss. Which is why you are going to want to find somebody who sticks to his routine and still generates impressive results.

4. Not afraid of Risks. You also do not want to choose somebody who is too scared of taking a risk. Most security investments are filled with risk. With the right mindset and strategy, a good fund manager will look use his technique to get past the risk and generate a viable income. It is useless to choose a fearful fund manager. Although there is no harm with a little caution, too much fear will strip the idea of a good investment. The reason why you chose to run your capital towards mutual funds is the possibility of diversification to lower the percentage of risk.

5. Steadfast Process. Most mutual funds are planned for long-term investment. Most of the time, people put their money on mutual funds for their retirement and insurance as they grow older. While digging up the records of a fund manager, make sure you assess their ability to "play" your money in the money market for a long-term plan.

6. Cheap Assets Trading. When you get to choose between a top-performing manager and an out-of-favor manager, odds are, you would want to choose the low-performing fund managers. Why? As a start-up mutual fund investor, you are going to want a lower expense ratio. As we have discussed earlier, expense ratios, also known as assets trading expense are one of the disadvantages of mutual fund investing. In choosing a low-profile manager, you will get a lower expense for trading as well. Think of it this way; in court, choosing a famous lawyer is more expensive than somebody who is not famous but it does not mean that the famous one is any better. But before you choose, make sure he meets the other criteria.

7. Too much Trading can Kill. There are fund managers who are too greedy in the money market. They put very fund in

trading securities. Although some people think that this is effective, it is highly unrecommended. Remember, we discussed earlier that the taxes as a disadvantage. When a fund manager has a turnover of 100 percent, the funding may be in trouble. He might not realize the loss incurred at the beginning of the investment. But if he gets greedy in trading, the expenses start to kick back when the capital gets hit by the tax bill.

8. Stick to the Small Ones. If you are going to choose between a fund manager who attracts a lot of clients and those who do not, choose the latter. A fund manager needs to focus on his job. If he takes too many clients, this could compromise the reliability of his performance. Think of it as the work of a social worker. If he works on multiple cases at a time, he might overlook details about his clients, and will not be able to focus on their needs.

9. Trust your Instincts. I know this can be a long shot in the dark, but your gut is a very important tool in investing. Sometimes, trusting our instincts is one of the best plays we do in business. Listen to your gut if you are uncomfortable with something. Because trust me, there is a reason why we feel doubt or worry. It could something we observed, felt, saw, or heard. You will never know whether you're right or wrong unless you follow your instinct. But usually, your instinct works great to ward off unwanted service in the business.

10. Seek Advice. Lastly, you will need to seek advice from experts. If there are meetings or seminars about any business-related facets, join and ask questions. Be one with fellow investors so you could learn a thing or two from their experiences. Maybe they can recommend some actions or

agencies that can help you. You never know, maybe you will have found the right fund manager at one of the conventions. Try to keep an open mind about every opportunity. It won't hurt to listen. At least you will know some prospects.

Chapter 4

Managing a Mutual Fund Investment

Everything you do to achieve success in your life, you do all by yourself. There is no shortcut and no proxy. You need to do everything by yourself. Even when you have financial advisors or financial managers, you still need to put an effort into your investments. When people think about business and investments, they usual think why they still need to work hard on their investment to be more profitable. Isn't the whole point of investing in mutual funds to be not working at all? Well, this is the biggest myth that people believe when it comes to financial investments. If you really want to be a successful entrepreneur, you will need all the power and resources you can harness to make your dreams possible. As a responsible mutual fund investor, there are certain things you need to do to actively manage your investment.

First and foremost, you need to be updated on everything related to your investment. Whether it is about taxes, the economy, deflation rates, inflation rates, stock markets, the rate of return, even environmental calamities - you need to be aware of the necessary changes and fluctuations. Keep track of everything that might affect the status of your investment. Do not just rely on your financial advisor or your financial manager to gain more profit. Remember, you're in it for success as much as they are. No matter how expert they are at their line of work, they are only human. There will always be things they do not know that needs to be researched. To work with them with full power, you must also have the initiative to function in a team.

I would like to enlighten you more about the need for team play through a simple illustration. We all know that the backbone of our economy is our farmers. Without those who sow and reap crops that we need for our daily survival, we will not be able to work at our full potential to serve our country. Without farmers, our economy is doomed to fail because there's no way to provide our basic human needs.

Much like in mutual funds, you are the farmer who provides everything to your investment and sees it prosper. All you need to do is gain knowledge on how you can manage your mutual fund's investment and apply it in real life.

Once you get an in contact with your financial manager and advisor, they will be creating a plan for your investment. Be it a three-year plan or a ten-year plan, you will begin to invest regularly. Of course, you will not be forced to pay a huge amount of money every month. You can choose a plan that allows you to invest while at the same time providing for your daily needs. When you invest regularly, you add more money to your capital, thus increasing the chances of earning a profit at the end of your saving plan. We have discussed earlier the disadvantage of pulling out your money ahead of time. You might encounter a loss and your investment will not be worth it. Which is why you need to develop a habit of regularly investing your money to avoid the occurrence of a loss in the long haul. Think of this as a saving method for your retirement. By the time you reach 60, will not have to worry about any financial difficulty. You can take your grandchildren and your great-grandchildren to school without a sweat. You can build a business that can run for generations after you have passed away. You can create opportunities for jobless individuals by hiring them into your firm.

Better yet, have your children inherit your legacy and let them work from there.

The second way to manage your investment is to constantly evaluate performance. You can do this monthly or quarterly with your financial advisor and your fund manager. Regularly check the status of your investment in the market and see how much you have earned and how much you have lost. When you evaluate your performance, brainstorm several ways on how you can increase it. Or better yet, think about how you can reduce the possibility of a loss. As we have discussed earlier, investments succeed through a series of trial-and-error methods. Work as a team and try different methods of investment vehicles. In that way, you can determine which strategy works out the best. In lieu of this goal, do not just rely on your team of experts when you can outsource to other people. Seek help from other professionals and gain their opinions about your prospects. In doing so, you can add some perspective on your goals and figure out more strategies to carry out.

One quick tip for managing your investment: as much as possible, pay your debts. Better yet, do not incur any liabilities. With everything said and done, you will want to focus on your needs and your investment. Having people tailing you around for your debts can derail you from establishing a stable viewpoint on your strategies in investment. Whatever expenses you have, pay them when they are due. Whether it is utility bills or small debts from a grocery store – Better sort everything before you engage in investment. You would not want any accrued interests to pay over on top of your need to invest for profits.

Be smart in grabbing opportunities. Maintain your discipline and tread wisely. You do not want to jump on the next investment just because it is "in" or most people say it is effective. Remember that times change, trends change, and markets change. Stocks from one company might have a high return on this day, but who is to say it will not fall tomorrow? Stay consistent on your goals. Never be too greedy nor too fearful in investing your money. Whenever you have doubts on an opportunity, consult someone about it. Do not engage without full information about any door that opens up for you. Not everything is worth trying. Some doors might even lead to our unfortunate downfall.

Chapter 5

How to Deal with Financial Loss

Success consists of going from failure to failure
without loss of enthusiasm.

Winston Churchill

An investment is easy when every step of the way you obtain profit. But it becomes a different story when you are dealing with loss. As a Start-up investor, you cannot expect to become an expert in a couple of days, even months. It takes time to become acquainted with the wisdom to make your own strategies and tactics in investing. Which is why you're going to need the help of financial professionals such as your fund manager and your fund advisor. In your years of living, you must have figured out by now that investment is a game of chance. No matter how good your colleagues are, there will always be factors that can affect your investment in the market.

The loss is an inevitable situation for all investors, especially those who are unaware and unguided. For most of them, the loss becomes the end of the line. It shows the finality of their strategies and the cessation of the whole investment. Incurring a loss challenges a person's integrity and enthusiasm in investment. That is, of course, when you let it beat you at your own game. See, even when you have incurred a loss, it does not mean that you can never make it back.

Failure is just a part of the process to learn and develop your skills as a person and as an investor.

Think of your financial losses as a challenge and to try to overcome it. It should not define your perspective and end game. Rather, think of it as the beginning of your milestone to success. You might not believe me if I tell you that losses are very vital tools to become successful in your investment. To this end, I will give you three illustrations on why losses lead to success.

Take for instance an athlete who trains his body to win a triathlon. During this process, he experiences lots of pressure and pain. He is forced to endure all forms of training to learn and develop his skills. He allows himself to be challenged physically, emotionally, and psychologically. Because he knows deep inside that these trials will make him a stronger and faster individual. No matter how many times he falls down on his knees, he knows that he needs to stand up, run further, and be better. Day and night, he puts his effort to himself in hopes that when the competition day arrives, he will be prepared to win. And he is confident to own it.

Another example is being a doctor. In the first years of a person's doctorate experience, mishaps are inevitable. I remember my cousin Jamie, a heart surgeon. During his early years of practice, I watched him stumble down and fall many times. Whenever he fails in one of his operations, he would break down and cry because of the guilt of losing a patient. I heard him say how he wants to quit his job because he feels worthless and incompetent in his line of work. If only he knew how much we admired his efforts with his patients, he would know that none of it was true. He started to lose sight of his goals and aspirations. He lost sight of what was important to the people around him. All he thought about was the fear of losing another patient. What he did not understand back then is the factors that have led to a person's death apart from his operation. For example, when the patient refused to undergo heart surgery until he found out of its terminality, there is a lower possibility that he could still survive. Sometimes, there are patients who are so hard-headed that they never do what the doctors prescribe until their condition becomes impossible to resolve.

After how many talks and interventions, Jamie decided not to give up after all. And I am glad he did not. He used these uncontrollable factors to influence his patients to do as the doctor recommends. As time went by, he became as confident as ever. He became one of those doctors who cared more than just earning a profit from patients. My cousin Jamie became an advocate for cardiovascular strength and has become an inspiration to many professional doctors.

Another profession that I would like to illustrate is that of a scientist. Think about Albert Einstein, Isaac Newton, and Rene Descartes. They were not able to create a scientific breakthrough overnight. It took them years before they could perfect their projects. Their theories and concepts were built over a series of trial-and-error methods. But even when they failed, they never stopped to believe in themselves and they never stopped to persevere.

Much like in business and investment there is no such thing as overnight expertise. It will take you months and years of hard work and determination. From the examples mention above, you can see that failure is a stepping stone to success because it allows you to learn from your mistakes and reflect on your actions. It makes you a bolder, stronger, and braver individual. The best part is that it makes you a wiser person ready to take on any challenge without losing enthusiasm.

For us humans, every time we encounter a challenge we are strongly affected. But to overcome our problems, we need to consider approaches that can help us sort ourselves out towards a more effective problem-solving and critical- thinking skills. Here are three commons coping strategies you can use to solve your problems efficiently:

1. The Appraisal-Focused Method

    This strategy aims to reframe the thinking or cognitive evaluation of a person towards the problem. Instead of thinking about it as the end of the world, a person needs to acknowledge that it is merely a challenge that needs to be solved. People have different perspectives. Some have imaginations that vary from the real context. This is the reason why the appraisal-focused method exists. A person needs to get in touch with the reality of the problem and not some mind-made assumptions of what it could be. If a person becomes apprehensive and pressured about all the possible and irrational outcomes, it would be difficult to discriminate which of those scenarios to focus on. To have a clear mind in solving various problems in investment, you need to clear your mind and identify the problem objectively.

    Once, there was an investor who put all his money in a start-up cooperative. He did not diversify his profits nor studied the factors that could affect his investment. He merely winged his money and assigned the chairman to take care of his investment as he waited for results. As months went by, he checked on the status of his money and found out that the cooperative had experienced a fatal fall and might be returning the investments of their clients plus the interests they accrued for seven months.

    To this, the man became furious at the cooperative for being incompetent and inadequate for service. He tried to file a complaint to the supreme court for negligence and had spread the word to people not to invest in the cooperatives for their vile work. He even exposed the names of the chairmen to humiliate them. But when he filed a complaint to the justice secretary, he only received a letter stating that the cooperative did not do anything illegal that could have caused their downfall. It was just a mere mishap due to the said uncontrollable factors that may not have been averted. Because of his actions, he fell into his own sword as it led the cooperative to file a complaint about libel and slander.

He did not listen to the explanation of the chairman for the loss and he neglected to understand the underlying reasons for bankruptcy. Because of his rash actions, he was charged to pay the cooperative an amount much higher than his investment plus interest for seven months.

From this story, we can learn the value of rational thinking rather than impulsiveness. To avoid making rash decisions after hearing bad news, it is always best to sort your thoughts out and think on how to solve the problem rather than who is to blame for it.

2. The Problem-Focused Method

This strategy is very important to fix the behavior of a person towards a problem. It is crucial to assess the strategic planning of your fund manager and fund advisor. Focus on the behavior that needs to be changed and work your way from there. In our previous example, that man needed to change how he dealt with problems. He needed to employ healthy ways of blowing off steam rather than humiliating people, even if they were not innocent.

3. The Emotion-Focused Method.

It is true when they said, "Do not let your emotions cloud your judgment." Whenever you make decisions, make sure you are not angry nor frustrated. Most of the time, the actions we make when we are emotional are the worst. We could regret it for the rest of our lives. Which is why you need to calm down before thinking about solutions. To make your decisions wisely, it is always best to have a stable mood and a sane temperament.

How to Deal with a Loss

In the professional perspective, there are various ways to neutralize or get back from a financial loss. It starts by following these five simple steps to deal with it altogether with your financial manager and your financial advisor.

Learn to Accept

The first thing to do when you have realized the loss is to accept the situation. This can help you cope and solve your issues faster. Whenever you try to deny the situation, you are merely delaying the process of sorting out your decisions and reflecting on your actions. Internalize within yourself the occurrence of a loss. And instead of denying what is in front of you, get yourself together and start reframing your perspective for the better.

Here are some don'ts in the acceptance of a financial loss. First, never repress your feelings about the situation. Psychologists have found that people who repress their feelings and memories tend to be prone to depression[1]. It is important to have a good grip on your emotions to avoid acting out and projecting to other people. If you do not get in control of your impulses, you might harm people through harsh words and you might do something you will regret for the rest of your life. Never make rash decisions when you are upset. It is best to stay rational and calm in making big investment decisions.

---

[1] *Dombeck, M. Repression. Retrieved from https://www.mentalhelp.net/articles/repression/

Seek Help from Professionals

Talk with your fund manager and your fund advisor about this issue and brainstorm the possible reasons why this happened. Create a list of your past decisions and actions on your investment and work your way down. For each entry, try to reflect altogether the pros and cons of the strategy. From here, you can assess what went wrong and reflect on your actions to create a suitable intervention.

As a responsible investor, you can also spend your time with other professionals so they can share their insights about your problems. You can try to open up about your recent ventures in hopes that they can pinpoint which of those strategies went wrong. By having a productive conversation with experts and pioneers, you can learn a lot from their experiences. And it would not hurt to try a thing or two from the concepts and tactics you have heard.

Do your Inventory

To deal with a loss, learn to assess your assets and liabilities. Make a list and try to account for these aspects. How much do I have? How much do I owe? To whom do I owe money? Could it be paid through non-monetary means? How much income should I earn each month to keep my investment going and pay my debts at the same time? What about my needs? Do I still have enough money to fend for myself and my family?

Define and Create your Goals

Once you have identified your needs, it is time to create a step-by-step plan to recover lost money and gain more profit from your investment. Firstly, create a plan that can solve your debts. If you have a liability to pay, you might as well earn for it and make it a priority, especially those with accrued interests. You can decide whether to do extra shifts at work, get an extra job, or earn money through buying and selling. Whatever method you use, make sure you do not incur any further liabilities. And remember to pay your debts with integrity and honesty.

Once you have paid your liabilities, you have obtained a stable standpoint on your financial status. The next problem to solve is providing to the needs of the family, and at the same time provide the necessary additions to the investment. There are several companies who give grace periods to their clients. Try to look for an entity that provides such amenities. This can help you adjust your financial obligations and make ends meet.

The last things to consider are the strategies to employ over the next financial period. If you have assessed which tactics to revise or discard, you have a better chance of using a better strategy next time.

Do the Necessary Corrections

Finally, take action to solve your problems. Be strong to put up an intervention to yourself, your fund manager, fund advisor, and your financial tactics. Think of it as a stepping stone to a better investment. Remember, nothing is perfect. I will not assure you that your next plan is going to be successful this time around. But you will never know until you try. Consistent action is the only thing that can produce tangible results. Without it, nothing can be accomplished. So, swallow your fear and set your head straight up into fixing what was broken and regaining what was lost.

Loss on a Psychological Perspective

Dealing with financial loss can take a toll on your psychological health. You are lucky if you are born with the resilience to take control of your emotions and face your problems head-on. But there are people out there who deal with problems on a deeper level. In psychology, they have a concept that defines people who are extremely emotional. They are not necessarily depressed nor anxious. These people just feel things with more intensity. They feel sadness like grief. They experience happiness like ecstasy. These people can feel sudden shifts of emotion from one person to another and they empathize with people they get in contact to. In psychology, a person who experiences these situations is called a "Highly-Sensitive Person" or HSP[2]. Do not misunderstand, there is nothing wrong with these people. They are not crazy nor mentally-deranged. However, they are more prone than anybody to develop clinical depression and anxiety.

In relation to mutual funds investment, there are people who take loss more deeply than others. Often times, it leads to depression and paranoia. Which is why it is important to discuss the different ways to deal with loss from a psychological perspective.

Share your Feelings

Whenever possible, have some friends and family around to support you. You should not be alone in dealing with problems such as these. So, call some friends or family members over and open up your feelings to them. If it helps, they can distract you from your problems by taking you shopping, going to movies, traveling, or enjoying other activities together.

Sharing your problems with other people is a good way to release the pressure, frustration, anguish, and devastation. Incurring a loss could be very difficult to some more than others. It is important to let things go once in a while. Your close friends and family can uplift your spirit and encourage you to move on. They will push you to believe in yourself and not give up. Because that is the most important factor. Having someone to motivate and inspire you to reach your goals is needed to get over the fact of incurring a loss.

---

[2] Meindl, S. (2019). Highly Sensitive People and Depression. From http://highlysensitive.org/highly-sensitive-people-and-depression-overstimulation-may-lead-to-depression/

We all have different forms of coping. Some take more time, the lucky few are pretty much resilient. Never be ashamed to open your feelings up. They are your family. I am sure they can understand what you are going through. Instead of bringing you down, they can lift you up on the way to a full recovery.

Keep a Journal

When you invest in mutual funds, it is important to have a journal of your business decisions and strategies. To top this off, it is also effective to have a journal for your personal experiences as well. Experts have found that writing on a diary or a journal can help a person think, reflect, and recover. It allows you to rethink your decisions and at the same time bring your inner emotions out. When you write, your mind focuses on your deeper thoughts without even knowing it. And as you pour it out, you will suddenly feel the ease of comfort soothing from your heart. The advantage of keeping a journal is you can write literally anything without the fear of getting judged or criticized. You can be true to yourself and be clear about what you really want in life.

Learn to Rest

One of the main reasons for burnout and depression is restlessness. To avoid demotivation and distress in your path to a successful investment, you will need to rest your mind and body from time to time. If you need to maintain a job, learn to take a break and have a snack. If it is break time, take a short nap or get some coffee just to relieve the tension. Once you go home, it is advised not to bring any of your workloads with you. Take time to pamper yourself once in a while. Watch the news, get distracted, play some games, invite somebody over, and focus your time on your family. There is no use in making a huge living when you do not know how to live your own life. It will only cause illnesses and burnout. You will not be able to function well.

In addition, maintain a sufficient amount of sleep when you can. If you can sleep for eight hours or more, take that chance and be refreshed in the morning. Experts have found that sleep is responsible for brain and body regeneration. It helps organize thoughts and impulses and it refreshes the brain to prepare it for a new day.

Maintain a Balanced Diet

Did you know that eating nutritious foods can do wonders to your body? Having a balanced diet can help boost the happy hormone called "serotonin"[3]. It makes a person resilient in dealing with various life adversities and it has been found to boost somebody's mood in a positive way. Instead of eating junk food and oily foods, choose fruits and vegetables instead. Observe that every time you eat a couple of chips you feel bloated. Then, your mind starts to slow down and your body becomes sluggish. These unhealthy foods can make a person unproductive, pulling him straight towards procrastination.

To avoid having such instances, change your lifestyle by changing the contents of your refrigerator or food compartments. Take out anything that smells of junk and exchange it with healthier foods. You can consider buying tofu instead of fried chicken all the time. Buy fruits instead of buying Cheetos. Resort to chocolate rather than buying a bunch of fake sweeteners. These diet changes can and will cause a dramatic increase in positivity in your life.

Exercise Regularly

Exercise is known to boost the hormones called "endorphins" or feel good hormones. When a person sweats, he creates a good vibe that affects his

---

[3] McIntosh, J. (2018). What is serotonin and what does it do? From https://www.medicalnewstoday.com/kc/serotonin-facts-232248

whole day. So, if you want to lessen the onset of frustration and anxiety, it is important to have regular exercise. It doesn't have to be in a gym, as long as you put your efforts into staying fit, you are set to face the challenges in life without breaking down. Did you know that being physically fit is directly proportional to becoming a successful person? When a person is fit, he is more inclined to work harder and persevere better against all life adversities. If you have fitness goals, it works hand in hand with you for your career goals. It establishes drive and motivation to be productive and stay inspired to keep moving upwards instead of sitting idly by waiting for good things to happen. Exercise pushes you to grab every opportunity for growth and development that you can use in your road to a successful life.

If you are looking for fitness exercises to follow, there are applications on the android or apple stores ready to download. You can use this to plan for your fitness goals in a whole month. If you like, you can also resort to YouTube videos on routines and sets you can do every day to boost your mood towards a happy and productive day.

Learn a Hobby

Whenever you get the chance to learn new things, grab it and learn a new hobby. You should not confine yourself in your work or business alone. You must have something hidden within your sleeves – a talent, skill, or ability. Whatever it is, you owe it to the world to show it. During your free time, perform your hobbies, join clubs, try new activities. If you have to travel just to learn more, so be it. As long as you live your life and experience the beauty in it. When you do, you will become stronger in facing the trials life gives you. Having a hobby is a way you can hold on to life no matter how hard it is. When you start to live for your passions and happiness, no adversity will bring you down. In fact, you will start to think differently. Instead of looking at adversity as a form of a problem, you will see it as a form of learning.

Get in Touch of your Inner Child

Remember when we were children, we never experienced complicated issues like we are now. I believe the biggest issue we experienced before is the lack of candy from the store. It was our problem where to get more ice cream or junk food. The issues we had were built on small rivalries between our classmates, siblings, and playmates. But they were not enough to cause depression nor anxiety. It just felt like a healthy competition to learn things from. But as we grew older, things got more difficult. Our problems got worse and simple frustrations became sources of agony and depression. Can you remember how simple things were back then? Things were not complicated at all. To get in touch with your inner child, you need to learn to make things simpler. Avoid thinking too much especially about the things where you do not need to concern yourself. Think of yourself first. Although it feels good to give to people around us, it is important to leave some for yourself. Love yourself as much as you did when you were young. Because that kind of self-love will save you from a lot of pain and anger that life will give you.

Do you remember when we were young? We used to laugh at the smallest things. Even when our older siblings and parents did not agree, we actually thought Barney and the Teletubbies were amusing. The reason? We had a simpler eye back then. So, to get in touch of your inner child, access your simple eye and keep it straight towards things that really matter to you. As much as possible, never neglect to provide yourself the chance to have fun, laugh, bicker, and play. No matter how much people judge you for regressing. It is not for them anyway. It is for your own development and for your own good. Most people will agree with this concept. But if I may ask, why do you need to be so serious when you can have fun from time to time. Loosen up! Learn to joke around with people. And soon, you can see the wonders of bringing out the child in you.

Chapter 6

Diversification of Assets

"Never depend on a single income,
make an investment to create a second source."

Warren Buffet

A couple of years ago, I knew a person, let's call her Layla, who invested in mutual funds during her late twenties. The financial advisors from the firm advised her to do it earlier, but she remained a skeptic and critical about the thought of investment. So, she did not engage in any form of venture until I convinced her to do so. She told me about her financial duties and obligations. And I assured her that there was nothing to worry about especially that there are programs and plans suited for her lifestyle and cash flow. She was a widow and had two children. She figured she would need a lot of money for when her children grew up. This enticed her even more to acquire a mutual fund. For over ten years, she regularly invested her money to the firm in hopes to generate income. Luckily, her financial manager did great! After ten years of her investment, her two children were already in high school. One in Junior Year and the other in Senior Year prepping for college.

Over the years, she met with two of her oldest friends who had businesses of their own. One has her own line of handbags. The other friend has her own retail salon. This made Layla a little bit insecure. And so, she decided to take out the totality of her money from the bank and start a business. Her financial advisor and financial manager were not able to dissuade her from her decision because she was thinking irrationally, out of envy. So, she invested half of what she earned from the mutual fund investment into her own business. The other half, she saved for the tuition fees of her son and daughter.

She decided to create a firm for statisticians and researchers to help students in college and master's degree for their thesis and research papers. She quit her job just to manage the firm and she was very good at doing her job. At first, the money from the investment was enough to fill the capital needed for her business. She was able to pay taxes, salaries, equipment, and utilities. But she did not anticipate external factors that could affect her venture. As we all know, thesis and research papers in school are seasonal. There are semesters where subjects in research and thesis are not offered. During those six months, she did not expect that there would be no clients to entertain. There were a few customers for revision, but it was not enough to cover the expenses incurred during the financial period. And because of this, she experienced a loss on her financial statement. Eventually, the firm needed to cease because she no longer had the ability to finance the salaries of her workers.

In Layla's experience, there was nothing wrong in withdrawing your money from the mutual fund investment and put it into another business venture. The downfall of her assets resulted from withdrawing the whole amount of invested capital plus the totality of interest. This left her mutual investment dry and empty. Had she withdrawn a small amount for the capital for her small business and still kept investing in mutual funds, she would have enough money to fill the capital of her small firm in the succeeding financial periods.

For me, maybe the only reason to withdraw the total principal plus interest from an investment is in the event of retiring. When all you want to do is travel, live your life, and enjoy your remaining years, that is the time when you should withdraw all your funds. Spend it for your happiness and your loved ones'.

In this story, we can learn a life-long lesson in investment that involves spreading assets to minimize the risk of bankruptcy and loss in the future. In this segment, we will be discussing the science of **diversification of assets.** From the word itself, it means spreading assets into multiple investment vehicles. Be it stocks, bonds, treasury bills, or personal business, the main goal of asset diversification is to minimize the risk of investment. Take, for instance, if I had a total of $30,000, I would choose to invest in three or more investment vehicles depending on the situation. I would invest a portion to mutual funds, a portion to buy a company's stocks, and build my own business. In that way, if I ever fall on a wrong track in whichever investment, I am secure to have two more sources of income. And if I ever choose to invest in stocks, I would purchase from different companies and firms. So, if one goes down, I still have a few more to rely on.

Diversification is not just something investors do to store capital and generate income but it can also be a way to achieve your ideal investment. Did you know that experts all around the world claim that diversification is the most important tool to reach your financial goals in the future? To understand this, let's look at the different types of risk when it comes to investment. The first one, called UNDIVERSIFIABLE RISK is also known as systematic risk or "market risk". This pertains to the uncontrollable forces in the economy of a country or state. This includes inflation rates, deflation, exchange rates, political and market instability, war, and natural calamities. This kind of risk is inevitable and it affects your investment with or without diversification of assets.

However, we have the second type of risk called the unsystematic risk, also known as DIVERSIFIABLE RISK which is only applicable to the factors that affect a specific entity, company, and industry. This can be reduced by spreading your assets into multiple unrelated investment vehicles. This risk is the main reason why you need to diversify your assets. So, you can protect your investment and avoid the onset of bankruptcy and loss.

This is the reason why diversification of assets is highly recommended to all investors. Given the return on investment for each vehicle is smaller because of the smaller capital invested, you will have greater security when you diversify your assets. However, much like any other venture in business, asset diversification has its own set of disadvantages. You might want to take note of these shortcomings to keep a stable asset allocation.

Disadvantages of Asset Diversification

More Work Needed

Since you will be targeting multiple investments, it will take more time to research each and every one of them. You are lucky if you have your own set of information and the statistics of every investment vehicle viable in the market. But if you are a start-up investor and you want to diversify your assets, you will need multiple intel to assess which investment vehicles to choose. Even if you have a financial advisor, it would still be difficult to assess each and every probable line for diversification. Both of you need to up your game and work as a team harder in order to diversify your assets to eligible and competent investment vehicles. However, this will surely take more time and it will need much effort to accomplish effectively.

Reduces Quality

Diversifying your assets alone can be very misleading. Without proper information, you might be enticed to invest in vehicles that are not competent enough to handle funds, hence reduces the quality of investment. Without proper research and guidance, you are more prone to making harsh decisions and being impulsive in buying investment vehicles. You have to remember that there are investment vehicles directly connected to each other. And you know how some firms are; they have the power to persuade you into investing in multiple investment vehicles without telling you so. If this happens, when the whole firm experiences bankruptcy, all of your investment vehicle will go down along with it. This is one of the most dangerous instances you need to watch out for.

Market Risk

Diversifying your assets does not get rid of the financial risks. You still cannot control the rise and fall of the economy which still might greatly affect your investment. This is a common misconception among investors. Some claim that diversification of assets is a good way to acquire more income. Although in most cases it does, this does not necessarily mean it is applicable for all. There are factors that affect the stability and status of your money in the market. Diversifying your assets does not lessen economical risks. It only reduces the risk of loss and bankruptcy.

Expenses of Trade

As we have discussed earlier, there are expenses incurred in investment. Diversifying your assets will bring you more costs for the trading and selling of different market investment vehicles.

Bad Vehicles of Investment

Since diversification of assets puts you in risk of a lack of information about other investment vehicles, you are prone to making bad investments. Much like my friend in the previous story, she invested in a business that went bad. She was unguided so she was unable to anticipate various economic and environmental factors that could have affected her attempt for a successful business.

Inattentiveness to Assets

Having too many investments in your portfolio makes you lose track of your other investments. Sometimes, investors are pushed to sell their investments because they lose track of their improvements. Managing multiple investments at once is a lot of work. Other people think it's easy. But to maintain a stable status in the financial market, a person actually needs to put an effort to manage his investment and not just sleep while his money earns. You will need to keep track of every single investment and learn to manage the profit and loss incurred at the end of every financial period.

There are a lot of disadvantages to asset diversification but it does not mean that it is not effective. Proper diversification is the key to success. When you manage your money right, you will have a successful asset allocation in no time. In the following chapters, I will be discussing more viable ventures to diversify your assets and generate more income.

Chapter 7

Where to Diversify Assets

As we have discussed in the earlier chapters, there are various classes in the financial market to choose from. But when you diversify, you will need to spread your capital into different financial classes to reduce risk. In this chapter, I will be discussing some of the most common business ventures where you can diversify your assets and generate a load of income. I will be discussing the advantages and disadvantages, how to start, and how you can manage your capital in your ventures.

Invest in Your Own Skills

> *"Investing time in yourself is the only safe investment that will give you maximum return throughout life."*
>
> *Lyrikal*

When a person invests on his talent, he gains pride over his passion while generating income from it. Your skills are your number one foundation into a successful business opportunity. I know what you are thinking right now. You might feel like you are not good enough at anything or that you do not consider anything as your talent. Well, nobody is too old for anything much less to discover their skills. Even when you know you have a skill or a talent, your journey should not stop there. You have an endless chance to learn and develop your talents even more.

First, you need to have some self-confidence to start. It is not enough having to tell yourself you need to learn and improve. You also need to start believing in yourself and really committing to the idea of being someone special. Everybody has their own strengths. You just need to be strong enough to acknowledge it. Whatever it is, be it writing, speaking, painting, sculpting, and many more, I am sure you can unleash your full potential if you want to.

For some people out there, the idea of following your dreams and investing in yourself is a bad joke. You would often hear them rant about not generating income or eventually failing in that journey. But the truth is, the most successful people started by following their dreams and investing in themselves. Like for instance, actor and model Arnold Schwarzenegger; it was his life-long dream to become an actor in the United States but he did not have enough resources to in the beginning. All of the people around him thought negatively of his dream and wanted him to pursue a different path. But Mr. Schwarzenegger was not easily thwarted by nay-sayers. During his younger years, he invested his time and money to enroll in acting classes and join fitness clubs. Afterward, he persevered and took small roles, one after the other until he finally got enough to travel to the United States. After taking part in small movies and modeling, he finally got promoted to the big screen as the star of *Terminator*.

The point is, you can make your passion your occupation. In that way, you can truly enjoy your life to the fullest. To invest in your talents, you need to provide yourself with the opportunity to learn and express your skills. Keep practicing and keep improving. Participate in community events to showcase your skills. Join competitions and ask for opinions from experts. Even if you fail or lose for the millionth time, never stop moving forward and making an effort to thrive. Learn from your mistakes and take criticisms constructively.

When you invest in yourself, strive to be the best you can. Not only will you acquire the courage to market yourself to the public, but you will also have the confidence to take and overcome one challenge to the other.

Do not hesitate to grab any chance to learn. Hire a coach, join a seminar, interact with fellow experts, read educational books and many more. Finally, you can use your assets into pursuing your talent and accomplishing your bucket list. Who knows? By this time next year, you could be a sensation and your name could already be written at the back of a hard-bound book.

However, investing in yourself is not always a walk in the park. There will always be challenges, shortcomings, and mishaps. For example, you might not anticipate various environmental and economic factors that can affect the marketing and production of your talent. Plus, pursuing your passion and investing in your talents can be a lot of work considering the steps you need to accomplish to establish your name as an expert. You will spend more time in advertising and promoting yourself. Not to mention the battle in the talent world is barbaric and a dog-eat-dog competition. It would be very hard to keep your head up high considering the factors that may bring you down. But if you persevere and be true to your passion, everything will fall into place.

Real Estate

> *"90% of all millionaires become so
> through owning real estate."*
>
> *Andrew Carnegie*

Another common form of diversification of assets is through real estate. Although this could be more complicated than other investment vehicles and self-investment, it could generate a lot of income for you. The process of real estate investment refers to the acquisition or purchase of multiple pieces of real estate in hopes to generate more income either through buying and selling or through a lease.

Firstly, if you plan in generating income through buying and selling, the process is way more costly and it takes a significant amount of time to generate income. This includes purchasing a less desirable structure or building and renovating it to a high-quality edifice that could attract buyers or businessmen. Once the improvement has been finished, you are now ready to sell it at a higher price. Therefore, generating profit from the beginning capital and expenses incurred during the process.

However, if you are using your building for lease, the process is almost the same. But this time around, it is less costly and it entails a lower amount of time to generate income. Plus, imagine if you have numerous tenants in the building. You can earn loads of money every month. Not to mention if you have offered a lease for the franchise, you can make a significant amount of return on investment before the year is over. But before your building is ready for rent, you need to make the necessary renovations and improvements to make the rooms ready for your clients. You can choose whether to make it a residential building or a franchise building for various business ventures. The next challenge to face is the building's registration to the city, paying the taxes, paying the bills, and paying for other maintenance expenses. Having a real estate for rent entails a faster cash flow rather than having it for sale.

Diversification of assets towards real estate is ideal for people who have renovating skills and social skills for marketing or dealing with tenants. If you are extroverted and you want to diversify your money into a business, real estate is the go-to investment. However, you need a healthy amount of capital to cover up every expense incurred in the process. If you have numerous connections in the market, then this could be the best way to diversify your assets. You have people to support your venture, and at the same time, they can help establish the name of your building to the public to generate popularity and promotion to prospective customers and tenants.

This investment is also applicable to people in investment groups. If you want to own a real estate and earn income without the effort of running it, constitute a group of investors who will run the properties hand in hand with you. This will lessen the load and the pressure of handling such a piece of building and getting to manage it on your own. Real estate could also be used for Trust Funding or Real Estate Investments Trust (REIT's). This refers to providing capital to a firm or a group of people who aim to buy and sell, or renovate and lease buildings for profit. It will be like investing your money into corporate shares, except they are individual contractors who aim to invest in real estate. This can help you generate income through profit shares every month or however you and the landlords see fit.

There are other countless ways to invest in real estate but the aforementioned are the most common. Of course, there will always be risk in whatever venture you choose to diversify your assets. Which is why you need to learn as much as you can before you decide to invest your money into real estate.

Disadvantages of Investing in Real Estate

1. It is a hands-on investment. If you plan to acquire real estate as an individual contractor, it could be very difficult to manage on your own considering the complex process when it comes to renovating and improving the building. This could be difficult to accomplish if you have a job and a family, especially when none of you are experts in

architecture nor carpentry. You are going to need manpower from agencies or other firms to help you improve the structure. And you are going to have to do all the research and promotions alone.

2. The process is costly. The expenses of renovating real estate entail a lot of money. Unless you have enough capital, your real estate investment is bound to fail. Not to mention you need to pay for overhead expenses to compensate for bills, utilities, taxes, and maintenance issues.

3. The process is timely. If you have tried building your own home, you can understand how renovating real estate can be very time-consuming. It can take months before you can furnish the structure to be ready for selling or rent. So, you need to ready yourself for months of nothing but outward cash flow. You cannot generate income unless you have finished the building and sold it or once you have enticed tenants to pay their monthly bills. However, you also need to account for the time when there are no prospective clients nor customers. For example, during vacation and summer break, it is common for people to go to their homes and spend time with their family. You also need to account for unforeseen events such as the death of a tenant, sudden move of tenants, and other situations that can compromise the cash flow of your business.

4. Depreciation of the building. As we have discussed in the earlier chapters, depreciation is the reduction of the value of an asset. This is also applicable to your estate properties. Take for instance, for many years, you have owned the real estate for lease then decided to sell it and buy another one. You need to take into consideration the depreciation expense and other economic factors that can affect the price of a building in the market.

5. Tenants can give you a headache. If you ever decide to rent your real estate, watch out for other tenants because they could be such a nuisance to you and their neighbors. There are those who seem responsible in the beginning, but once they have been approved for a lease, they may become neglectful of their duties as a tenant. This includes not paying their rent for months. This could leave you at the disadvantage of always running after them for their payment. And once they decide to leave the room without notice, it could take a toll on your financial status in holding the real estate. You are going to need every amount of money power to pay for your dues as a landlord. Having irresponsible tenants can really affect the cash flow of your venture.

6. Increased liability over shortcomings and accidents. There are events when the landlord is held liable for accidents like unstable floorings, faulty showers, and slippery floors. Even when the owner did not have anything to do with it, he needs to take account for every liability and shortcomings that ever occurred inside the building. There are times when the landlord is obliged to pay for hospital bills and other medical related bills because of the "findings" or results of the investigation.

7. Real estate is a non-liquid asset. In cases of emergency, you need to remember that real estate is not readily convertible to cash. You cannot sell it the moment you experience a fatal mishap. The only fund source available is those from the rent expenses paid by the tenants. In the case of real estate buy and sell, it could be very difficult to sell a building especially with the lack of connections and popularity.

Simple Hacks

1. Consider the place. In choosing a real estate, you need to take in consideration the place of the investment. You would want to buy a piece of real estate where there are schools, job opportunities, and workers who are looking for a place to stay. You would want to buy a real estate near or in the city to make sure you generate traffic into your building for lease.

2. Consider the culture. Most of you might think that there could be a variety of cultures present in a certain society. How come culture matters in real estate? To increase the rate of success in the acquisition of real estate, you need to take in consideration the common preferences of the majority and renovate your building in such a way that people are enticed to stay at your building. Having real estate that matches the taste of the majority can boost your reputation as a viable and eligible place to live in.

3. Factors affecting the economy. In starting a real estate investment, you also need to consider the environmental factors that can affect your integrity as a well-established landlord. Take into consideration the changes in the weather, and the extremity of calamities. You need to assure people that they will be safe inside your humble walls if ever there are earthquakes or typhoons. Assure the people that you have everything they need in short notice like emergency kits, fire hydrants, air conditioners, and many more. If you intend to be more famous, you can make an imprint on society by giving them something they need like a conference hall, a gym, a pool, or anything available for a social gathering. This can up your game as an effective service provider to society.

4. Competitors. You must often think about your competitors in your area. Think about a way you can be different and

unique from your competitors. What do you offer that they do not? Is there a unique style of the building? Do you have amazing food? Do you have affordable prices? Think about everything that can overpower your competitors to rise up to the public as the best.

However, competitors could be detrimental to your popularity especially when they have established their name ahead of time. Putting up with expectations of people can be very difficult, especially in promotion and advertising. Which is why you need to know and assess your competitors to determine which strategies to implement to become successful as a landlord.

1. The reputation of the building. Do not purchase a building which has a bad reputation to the public. Whether there was a breach of security in the past or it was haunted, as much as possible do away with those kinds of buildings because it can affect its future reputation no matter how renovated it might seem. Although it does not necessarily apply to all, in places where people are superstitious, it could be a big factor.

When I was a child, I always knew this building, let us call it the Hotel Dutchman. During the 1980s, it was one of the most glorious hotels ever made. My mom would usually tell stories about it. Lots of tourists were enticed to stay at Hotel Dutchman during the holidays. But one night, there was a kidnapping outside the hotel. The doorman and the security guards were forced to call for the police and avert the situation. Of course, the people inside the building were nosy and curious about what was happening outside. Civilians were shouting and yelling the kidnapper to let go of the innocent lady. When the police came, it became an incident of "rescue went wrong". When the police were pointing every gun to the culprit, he panicked and shot himself to death. The story was told from one generation to the other, leaving the Dutchman Hotel abandoned.

Every time we walked past this structure, we had chills and we were forced to run without any apparent reason. I remember one time, my friends and I were on our way home from school. One day, somebody finally bought the rights of the building and it was renovated for rental. Many business owners were attracted to the new building, so they rented rooms for a franchise and other business ventures. The downside was that the reputation of the building still remained in the society. Whenever people would go and do their business inside the building, they would tell the tale of the culprit who took his own life. This story spread like wildfire to the tenants of the building. Although I do not believe in ghosts, some people have claimed they either saw spirits or they feel hauntings inside the building. I don't know if it was psychological because of the stories or it is phenomenal because it is real. The point is, the reputation of the building remains and it could be a factor to consider in some parts of the globe.

Choosing a Real Estate Broker

I know, most of you might not be an expert in real estate yet which is why you are going to need a real estate broker to help you search for a viable building or help you sell a renovated one. Much like looking for a fund manager for a fund advisor, there are also tips to consider in choosing a real estate broker.

1. Follow your instinct. Sometimes the best brokers are found using the gut of a person. When you meet up with somebody, there is this sudden question, "Am I going to like this person or not." Seconds after meeting him or her, you eventually have the feeling whether you can trust him or not. This basic instinct is true most of the time. But of course, it is our duty

to give the person the benefit of the doubt. Apart from our instincts, we need to get to know the person professionally but at the same time take into consideration the feelings you have in choosing a real estate broker.

2. Meet and greet at seminars and workshops. To gain insights on potential brokers, you can try to join seminars and meet experts. From there, you can ask for competent real estate brokers. Who knows? Maybe you can find the right broker for you in those kinds of events. Plus, you can learn various lessons and hacks in real estate investment from experienced individuals. You can ask around about their strategies and techniques to obtain a successful real estate.

3. Do not be afraid to interact with the professionals. They remember what it is like to start and they know how difficult it is. Which is why you need the confidence to reach out to them for help. Feel free to ask them, "Where should I start? How much money do I really need? My goal is this… what can I do to make it better? All of the things that bothers your mind, you can ask during these meetings. This is the main reason why people host seminars and workshops so people can learn. To make a good run for your money, learn as many as you can in the art of real estate investment.

4. Ask for referrals. If you have friends and family members who have experience in real estate, you can ask for names of competent real estate brokers. But be careful if you have a "friend" who says that he or she is a legitimate broker. Before you believe them, make sure you do your own research about their past clients and business ventures. Do not let the spirit of friendship break a successful streak of investment. If you ever find out that he or she is not competent enough to be your real estate broker, then let the person down slowly and respectfully.

5. Once, there were two siblings who went their separate ways only to work with each other in the future. Of course, there will always be faith and trust among siblings. That is something that does not wear off over time. The eldest child was a real estate investor, while the younger one was a real estate broker. When they met during one of the conferences, they eventually decided to work together as a team to find real estates to buy and sell. The older brother did not do any background investigation on his sibling. Little did he know that he was fired from his past firm for being careless in his job. He only enticed his big brother through the lies he fed him. It was too late when the investor found out that his sibling was a scam artist. He lost millions of dollars because he let his "broker" spend it in low-quality buildings which were far away from the city. How can you convince other investors to buy such buildings for rent if there is a lower population in its location? Not to mention that with the low market price and the high taxes, the older brother was left at a loss.

6. So, always remember to make your own investigations to potential real estate brokers, be it a family member or a friend. You need someone that does not compromise the integrity of your investment in the market.

7. Do your research on your prospective brokers. Before you choose your prospects, make sure you do your research ahead of time. Who are they and what is their expertise? What are their skills and how good are they in marketing and strategizing towards a successful business? These are the things you need to account for in looking for a real estate specialist.

8. Look for somebody who understands what you need. Your real estate broker must have the ability to empathize with you

on your dreams. You must have an effective way of communicating and understanding each other because this is a vital key to building a good real estate investment. Do not choose somebody who imposes himself and his preferences as your decision. He must be sensitive to what you want and what your real estate would look like. He must be willing to suggest ideas and concepts without sounding greedy or boastful towards himself.

9. Look for somebody who gets paid out of the performance. Much like looking for a fund manager, you need someone who can put his utmost effort to the success of your investment. Look for a broker who gets his incentive from a good work, not somebody who gets paid whether or not he succeeds. Some of these people have the tendency to slack off and take your investment for granted.

10. Check previous records and inventory. Once you have narrowed your search to a few brokers in your area, it is time to check their past projects and inventory. Look for good records in the past year. But you need to do this critically. Do not let one mistake or bad project dissuade you from hiring a broker. There are many factors that could have affected the fall and success of a real estate investment.

11. Check for good values. As much as possible, look for a real estate broker who is passionate, determined, honest, and trustworthy. You can assess a person through talking and interviewing. From there, you can ask how they feel about your opinions. You can also pretend to sound ignorant at the beginning to see how patient they are in explaining and dealing with people who are ignorant in the concept of real estate. It also helps to ask them questions you already know the answer to. This is not for the purpose of mockery. Rather,

it is to assess the value they put into their work. It shows their persistence to see their future projects succeed.

12. Check for risk mitigation. It can also help if you ask them how they feel about risk. Choose somebody who can avert risk or somebody who can assure minimal to zero risks. Unlike mutual funds investment, as much as possible, avoid taking high risks in real estate. Remember, this is a non-liquid asset. When you have made a mistake, it is difficult or impossible to avert especially when you plan to buy and sell. Of course, the journey towards real estate is a dog-eat-dog competition so you need the best of the best to show the world. Having something "good enough" is never really enough in the expectations of the public.

13. Look for realism and honesty. Look for a real estate broker who does not beat around the bush especially when making big decisions about the investment. You need somebody who says their opinions loud and clear. For example, when you are about to make a bad decision, you need somebody to stop you from committing a mistake. You need someone to hear the negative along with the positive. Avoid somebody who loves to sugarcoat things because it usually does not result in anything good or productive.

Buy and Sell

"The wisest rule in investment is: when others are selling, buy. When others are buying, sell."

Jonathan Sacks

Shopping is one of the most common forms of stress relief, especially among women. After a long, hard day, some women would go to malls and check out the new edition of makeup, shoes, dresses, watches, shades and more. There is an undying need to shop even if a person already has enough garments. Plus, trends and fads change from time to time. Preferences change and perceptions change. Which is why the market is a never-ending process of innovating, designing, creating, and discovering.

In this generation, buy and sell is the most common form of business. When it comes to the diversification of assets, most investors choose to purchase assets at a lower price and sell it for a higher price. The concept of buy and sell is actually quite simple; buy low and sell high. You can choose any asset really, from clothes to accessories, to appliances, cars, motorcycles and many others. It is solely up to you how to strategize in your society. But we will get to that later. For now, let us discuss the beauty of the buy and sell for investment.

For those of you who have high marketing and social skills, this could be one of your best investments yet. As long as you know how to entice people into buying your product, you are good to go. One advantage of the buy and sell is having a clean income out of your sales. If you are the sole proprietor of the assets, there is no division of profit among your co-owners. The only thing you need to finance is the capital you will use to buy assets at a low price, the shipping fee of the assets to and from your inventory, the necessary taxes paid to the government for registration if there are any, and the rent and overhead expense just in case you decide to open up your new store.

There are two ways to run a buy and sell – to do everything hands-on or to finance people to handle it for you. If you have a job and you have no time to handle the business, you can hire some assistants, probably some friends and relatives to help you buy and sell assets for profit. But if you want to do this full-time and establish your inventory at home, then you can save the salaries expense and the rent expense for other purposes.

Anyone can venture in buy and sell because this is one of the few viable investments with minimal skill requirements. You can literally work from home and gain profit on a regular basis. Buy and sell is one of the most recommended ways of asset diversification because it entails minimum risk and minimum cost. Of course, there are instances when assets turn out to be of poor quality. You can just make the necessary corrections and top up the price to gain more profit anyway. Another good thing about buy and sell is the wide market. You can literally sell all over the world given you strategize methods into catching people's attention into your products. Plus, you have a pricing advantage. So, even when you offer your merchandise at a lower price, you can still earn a profit because of the money you save from all other expenses.

Buy and sell has been revolutionized ever since the breakthrough of social media and the internet. You no longer have to knock from door to door just to convince potential customers. All it takes nowadays is Facebook, Twitter, Tumblr, eBay, and other selling platforms. What you need to do now is generate enough traffic to establish your name and products to the public.

However, you need to remember, like any other venture in business, buy and sell has its shortcomings and disadvantages too. When you decide to diversify towards buying and selling, you really need to commit your time and effort to the management of your stocks. It is not just a buy, then hold, then sell strategy. It is the process of maintaining your goods and merchandise on a good condition. This includes proper packaging, proper stacking, proper conditions of storing, and many other factors. Especially when you plan to buy and sell food, clothes, or books, these should be stored in a secure and safe place away from any insect or pest that might aim to compromise its quality.

If you intend to have other people manage the business for you, it is difficult to look for people who are qualified to look after the merchandise and maintain their good quality. You need someone who has the ability to scrutinize quality and assess the merchandise as a top-most priority. Taking the stocking procedure for granted can cause the ultimate downfall of your buy and sell venture. Another risk in holding stocks of merchandise is the probability of theft and spoilage. You know how thieves are. They are very cunning and effortful to get what they want. When they figure out that you have a storage area filled with goods and merchandise, chances are, they'll aim to pilfer what they can for their own benefit.

Lastly, as discussed above, the preferences of the people can change in a heartbeat. Storing only one kind of merchandise can be detrimental to your financial status especially when you aim to obtain a regular income. Sometimes, it becomes impossible to track the changes in trends and fads in a society. Which is why you will need a variation of products to sell. To do this, you are going to need a higher amount of capital to start your business. So, how do you do that?

How to Start a Buy and Sell Business

First and foremost, you need to do your own research about the fads and trends in your community. What do the people need? What do they want? What is their culture? Consider these factors as a stepping stone to choose which products to purchase for reselling. It helps to gather knowledge from experts and professionals. If there are business tycoons present in your community, try to research the strategies they employed to make things a success. List your prospective items for purchase and assess one by one until you narrow it down to three. These merchandise, assets or commodities will serve as your starting point as a reseller. But do not put away your long list of prospective assets. Remember, the trends and fads change in a matter of days, weeks, or months. There is a possibility that you will be needing to change your merchandise from time to time.

When you finally rank the assets from the most viable to the least viable, it is time to dig a little deeper about the product and its status in the market. What does it really do? Who are your target customers? Who are your competitors? Is it a need or a fad? Is it a trending commodity in the market? When it comes to the product, you need to get to know the asset from the inside out. What does it do? How does it help people? Why should people acquire such an asset and what are its disadvantages? These factors are needed to help you advertise the product in the market and establish your name as an established seller. Of course, the consumers will ask multiple questions about your merchandise. You need to be knowledgeable and honest about it to avoid liabilities and other setbacks in your venture.

As much as possible, do not choose a product that everybody else sells. This will generate less traffic to your merchandise and it poses a risk towards untimely loss. When bigger companies have the same products, it could be difficult to keep up with people's expectations. It would be difficult to establish a trademark towards your name. Unless you have an innovative way to make yours better and attract the customers' attention, and unless you do not have any competitor in an area, do away with common goods. Why do you need to go with the flow if you can stand up from the crowd? If you are creative and can innovate your own product, then that would be a big stepping stone to a big business opportunity.

Once you have established your research among various products it is time to look around and canvass low-priced merchandise for reselling. You can visit garage sales and thrift stores for huge sales. From there, you can acquire multiple goods and sell them for a higher price. But you need to remember, in choosing dry goods, choose products with good quality for easier reselling. You would not want your customers to see low-quality products sold at a higher price. That could take a toll on your reputation as a seller. In addition to this, look for places and stores where you can buy in bulk. Some stores offer huge discounts to people who buy in bulk. Take this opportunity and resell the products at a higher price for greater profits. To have a little more insight about the business of buy and sell, here are some factors to consider before you start:

1. Licenses and permits. To avoid legal issues, it is important to establish a legal permit or license for selling. This is usually required when you want to step out of your home as an inventory space and create a bigger business in buy and sell.

2. Taxes. This goes hand in hand with your business registration. The taxes paid refers to the mandatory financial charges imposed by the government to fund necessary public expenditures. The tax rate varies from one region to another. Sometimes, it could rise and fall due to various economic factors that can affect the market.

3. Shipping and Delivery. You need to remember that not all couriers are the same. If you plan on reselling fresh fruits, vegetables, and other perishable goods, there are specific carriers to hire apart from the typical couriers that draw restriction lines in the locality. Also, if you intend to ship internationally, you need to consider the shipping fee per location to avoid loss.

4. Trademark, Copyright, and Patents. If you intend to make your own products for selling, it is important to secure the trademark, copyright, and patent of your products to secure its authenticity and to avoid the risk of other people stealing your work. You can ask for the Department of Trade and Industry in your region to assign the exclusive rights of your design and product solely to you.

5. PCI Compliance. This protects eCommerce sellers from data theft. If you aim to use business platforms, it is best to comply with the requirements. This ensures security to your assets and your inventory by preventing various forms of a security breach.

6. Age Restrictions. There is a guideline for every online business owners to comply with COPPA, also known as the Children's Online Privacy Protection that aims to protect the personal information of individuals under 18 years old from any form of issue.

7. Insurance. There are instances when liabilities seem to be inevitable such as product liabilities, commercial liabilities, marketing, and professional liabilities. To avoid such problems in your venture, you are going to need insurance for these factors. For example, there has been an accidental breach from quality control on your part and the product has already been delivered to the customer. As a responsible owner, you must have the insurance of changing the damaged goods. Also, when you intend to use shipping, you must ask for insurance from your provider in cases of mishaps and accidents. Whenever your goods or products have been damaged due to careless transportation, the courier must be held liable to pay for the price of your merchandise.

How to Sell Products in the Market

This is the most commonly asked question when it comes to buy and sell. Of course, there are many different ways to sell aside from one-to-one communication. But in this venture, communicating with your customers is a vital tool to really sell your products and rank up your name in the community market. But before I discuss how you should speak to your potential clients, let me tackle the characteristics you need to develop to furnish your communicating and persuading skills.

1. Empathy. In order to gather the attention of your customers, you need to show them how much you care about their concerns. You need to learn how to listen avidly to their thoughts and feelings. Plus, you need to show them that you feel their emotions as much as they do. In doing so, you can build rapport to your clients and establish a trust for further transaction.

2. Competitiveness. When customers open their mind to you and your products, show them how much you care about your business. When consumers feel that the products and the business is taken for granted, they are dissuaded to go into any other ventures with you. You need to show your knowledge and skill in showcasing your products to give them the impression that you know what you are doing and you have familiarized yourself with the product by heart. The information you hold regarding your products is a plus point for your efforts and tenacity. It means that you are responsible for handling your merchandise and you are willing to do anything to take good care of it while it is in stock.

3. Commitment. Show your passion and fervor toward your business. As much as possible show them that you love what you do and you are not only doing this for money. Assure them that you have engaged in the buy and sell venture because you want to provide the needs and wants of the people in society. It is not enough to show good products to your customers. You also need to show that you uphold your societal responsibility by promoting quality, innovation, and trustworthiness.

4. Honesty. Your consumers are smart and intelligent people. They are very diligent in doing their own research about various products. Sometimes, some customers are even more knowledgeable than you about the product and they still ask you questions they already know the answers to. There are customers who will test you for your knowledge and expertise about the product. Given, there could be information you do not know yet. All you need to do is be honest about it. Never false-advertise. If you do not know any side effects, respectfully tell your buyer to keep caution. Do not merely say there are no side effects or disadvantages. Given they get sick from your products, you will be held liable for the expenses. You would not want that to happen to you. This usually happens when selling cosmetics, vitamins, and food. But if you are selling dry goods and other merchandise, tell your customers if there are any dents, damages, or shortcomings of your product. Attracting your customers through deceitful means is detrimental to your business. And all your immoral acts will eventually catch up to you.

5. Curiosity. Never neglect to improve your knowledge in your line of work. You should have a burning need to know more about your products and your market. It is not enough to say that you know so much already. There will always be room for improvement and growth. Stay curious about concepts and theories that may come in handy on your venture towards buying and sell. Do not disregard simple suggestions and advice from people because there are reasons why they say such things. Maybe it came from their own experiences or the experience of other people. What matters is you stay inquisitive about everything whether you think it is valuable or not. It does not hurt to listen. In fact, it is a good way to learn new things and advance to a whole new level.

6. Humility. As a seller, you need to remember to stay humble and do away with greed. No matter how successful you have become, it is important to keep up a humble feature and show your clients that you are an approachable person. Once they feel how understanding and down-to-earth you are, they will be more enticed to patronize your products even more.

7. Consistency. You also need to show your customers that your efforts are undying towards your business. Your zeal and commitment must be burning at all times. Being inconsistent in your decisions and actions can dissuade your clients into looking for other sellers to patronize. Your consistency as a seller is a very vital tool to attract customers into believing that you can be trusted and that your products are of high-quality.

8. Patience. Of course, there are also potential clients who are ignorant and unknowing of the nature of your products. And let us face it, some people can understand better than others. And there are those who are hard to deal with. But you are going to need every potential customer there is. So, to attract these clients, you need to show them patience and fervor in explaining to them what they need to know. They need to feel that you care about them as much as you care about your products. When they feel like they are being prioritized, your name will be spreading around the community like wildfire. More people will advertise your services and many people will start to prioritize you as a viable seller.

Now it is time to get into the good stuff – how to talk your customers into buying your products. When somebody knocks to your door and endorses their own products, what do you like to hear? And what don't you like to hear? I want you to list these things on a piece of paper. For example, if I was to knock on your door and sell you kind of supplement. What are the things you want to hear that might persuade you into buying? Is it the brand, the reviews, the benefits, or other factors? What are your pet peeves? Is it the time it takes for them to endorse or the manner of speaking?

Well, all of these play a role in persuading a customer into buying your products. First and foremost, you first need to feel the emotions of your prospect. Is he in a good mood? Is he busy? From his surroundings or facial expression, what do you think he needs? From here, you can start to build a rapport by asking how they are holding up. Allow them to open up their emotions. Let them share how tired they are after a long work, and let them share some of their problems with you. Sometimes, it helps to be empathetic to people with a lot of problems so they can clear their head and focus on your endeavor. Next, establish your standpoint in a manner they can perceive the solution to some of their problems. To do so, remember to limit your endorsement to a maximum of 60 seconds unless you are given permission to continue. In those sixty seconds, you need to fit the information: What is your product? How is it used? When was it found? Why do the customers need your product? After that minute, allow the potential customer to open his opinions about the product. Push them to speak frankly about their thoughts towards the product. Encourage them to ask questions and reveal their inner emotions. During this phase, show them that you can listen avidly and you empathize towards their emotions. Avoid sounding sarcastic or discouraged despite their means of communicating. Employ the techniques of active listening such as staying attentive, making eye contact, open body language, asking questions for clarification, acknowledging feelings, restating their words, and giving nonverbal feedback like smiling and nodding.

When the customers seem agitated, stay silent and listen to their concerns. Never talk back to avoid negative feedback on your portfolio. Soon thereafter, they start to realize their mistakes and realize they are extremely wrong for doing so. When they ramble on and on about things non-related to your business, or when they start to exchange unnecessary and hurtful words, cut the conversation politely. And end your venture by saying, "I am sorry for what you are going through. I can only imagine the experience you are having right now. Maybe we can talk about this another time." Then, say goodbye.

But if the conversation goes well, you can continue with your product's benefits and reviews from people who have already experienced using it. Elaborate on the contents of your product if it is an edible good or a supplement, and explain the benefits of each. It is also helpful to bring before and after pictures of previous clients in a period of time. This helps entice a person to purchase goods especially when it is proven effective. Remember, the main reason why a person remains skeptical towards a product is their fear of ineffectiveness and its high price. So, you need to avert their worries by assuring them of the rate of effectiveness of your products.

Check their facial expressions and body language for hints of disapproval or misunderstanding and ask them if there are clarifications in a polite manner. It also helps to gather their opinion about your products to know how else you can persuade your client into buying your product. Never negate their opinions. Instead, assure them that you understand their concerns. Learn to bargain when you can. You can use the door-in-the-face technique where you put a high price to your product. Of course, your buyer will most likely reject it. This is the time when employing a huge discount to persuade your prospect to buy. If you think you can still afford to provide a discount, do so. This helps establish patriotism among your buyers. Especially when they perceive you can easily be approached and bargained with.

Once you have established your product well and there seems to be no more questions or clarifications from your prospect, you can end the conversation by asking, "Will it be okay to schedule another meeting at your most convenient time to show you more samples of our products?" If they agree, then you have a chance to show your prospect more of your products in the future. But if they reply otherwise, at least you tried your best to persuade him to buy your products.

Remember, there will always be people who are difficult to deal with. But do not lose hope. For if there are negative people, there are also more positive ones. All you need to do is look for them and give everything you got to persuade them. Also, the art of speaking and interacting with people takes a lot of practice. Nobody becomes an expert overnight. You can employ trial-and-error methods of advertising or gather a panel to assist you in developing unstoppable persuasion skills.

Assets Eligible for Reselling

1. Mobile Phones and Tablets.

2. Computers and Laptops.

3. Books and Publications.

4. Clothes.

5. Shoes.

6. Bags.

7. Cars.

8. Furniture.

9. Confectionaries.

10. Jewelry.

11. Supplements and Vitamins.

12. Event Tickets, concert tickets, and movie tickets.

13. Musical Instruments and other accessories.

14. Sporting Goods.

15. Watches.

16. Animal Breeding.

17. Antiques and Old Coins.

Second hands are the most common trading merchandise in buy and sell. For more expensive assets such as phone, laptops, tablets, computers, cars, and other machinery, you can purchase second-hand assets from certified retailers at a very low price. However, if you want to increase the status of your asset, you need to make the necessary fixes to have a reasonably high price in the market. A lot of people prefer second-hand assets because of the concept of wear and tear. Your consumers know for a fact that these kinds of assets degrade over time. And with the necessary repairs and fixes made, it would be like buying something brand new but at a cheaper price. You can observe the younger generation nowadays, they prefer to post something on Facebook that goes like this, "Looking for Laptop." On the comment section below, people would post their second-hand laptops with its specs at a cheaper price. From there, the customer takes his pick and starts to assess the asset further. Same is true with selling cars and motorcycles. Instead of going to famous companies and spending thousands and dollars for a brand-new car, they prefer to check for online hand-me-downs for a cheaper price.

For clothes, shoes, bags, and watches which are more common in the market, branded second-hands are very famous in online selling. Branded merchandise is too costly for famous malls and shops. When people buy online, they maximize their money by purchasing second-hand garments with the same design but a cheaper price. Do you want to know a secret? Most people prefer Class A and B merchandise because they can enjoy the quality and the design of the original merchandise but at a very affordable price. So, do not fret when selling Class A or second-hand garments. As long as it is of good quality, you are sure to have customers knocking on your door.

To have an instant sale of assets, you can resell event tickets or concert tickets. But you need to choose the best and most famous trend. In this generation, the most common concerts among generation are brought by One Direction, The Vamps, Five Seconds of Summer, Taylor Swift, John Legend, and many more. Almost all of the time, their tickets get sold out. But if you own the only remaining tickets to their concerts, their top fans will be willing to pay for the tickets, and you can just sell it to the highest bidder.

Animal breeding is also a famous way of earning money. This is the process of acquiring a pet such as a dog or a cat for breeding. When they reach their adulthood, they will be ready for breeding, and you can sell the offspring internationally. In the United States alone, animal breeding, especially among dogs, is very common. Breeds such as the Siberian Husky, American Bully, Rottweilers, Belgian Malinois, and the German Shepherd. There are also smaller breeds such as the Shih Tzu, Pomeranian, Corgi, and many others. Did you know that when you have established your name as a dog breeder, you can sell puppies for as high as 10,000 dollars? This is common among famous breeders of the American Bully. Their product is famous in an international sense. They even have customers from Europe, Spain, even the far east such as the Philippines. You would be surprised how establishing a famous name can influence your sales!

Antiques are also very common in the line of buy and sell. You can look for your old coins and sell it at a high price or to the highest bidder. You would be surprised how much collectors are willing to pay for such assets. If you can observe in the market, old cars made in the 1950s and 1960s are more expensive than brand new cars. The authenticity of these assets is priceless. And there are antique enthusiasts who are willing to give anything just to be in possession of one of these antiques. You can also resell old cameras, authentic furniture, and other antique garments in the market. It helps to visit garage sales and rush sales to see such cheap objects. Take advantage of these sales because other people's trash is golden in the market. You will never know what you can find until you go.

Old books and publications are also timeless in the market. As you can observe in book stores, limited edition books that were published in the early 1900s are very expensive. There are people who collect such assets as their hobby. Much like antiques, they're willing to pay for it at a very high price. You're lucky to find books published in the 1800s or 1700s, these books can cost quite a fortune in the market. Apart from these, the reasons why people look for second-hand books and publications is to save money from buying new and expensive books. Granted, some books might be outdated in nature but it doesn't mean that they are not educational. You would be surprised to find out that some adults are more inclined to buy old books rather than new ones because of their manner of writing, voice, and authenticity. Some people claim that people create books nowadays which are too overrated to read. I should know, when I was a student, I preferred reading older versions of books because of their simplicity. So, whenever there were book fares, I would entice my mom to come look for old textbooks as a reference for studying.

How to Set up Online Selling

1. Identify your target market. There is a great advantage selling online because of millions of potential customers. However, the rise of competition is not to be taken for granted. There will be thousands of companies worldwide fighting over the people's attention. Which is why it helps to identify a

specific target to amplify your efforts into enticing these potential customers to purchase your merchandise. For example, if you are selling clothes, what kind of clothes do you want to sell? Is it for young adults, teenagers, babies, and toddlers, or the elderly? If it is for teenagers, what fashion do you want to focus on? The chic type? The casual type, or any other fashion statements? You also need to understand the common hobbies of certain age groups to identify what they want and what they need.

2. Once you have an idea of the specific target of the population, gather as much information about them and figure out the change of trends in the market. What specific colors do they prefer? What designs would they most likely purchase from you? All of these things are important in generating more traffic into your merchandise.

3. Pick or create an e-commerce platform. There are hundreds of selling platforms to choose from. But to have a more effective marketing strategy, you need to consider these criteria for a viable and effective eCommerce platform.

   a. User-friendly. Avoid choosing a platform that is too complex. As much as possible choose an e-commerce factor where everything can be understood by just looking at it. For example, user-friendly platforms include a search button for specific needs and wants. It includes tabs for organizing one class of merchandise from the other. It could also include some buttons for sorting color and price to make it easier to canvas.

   b. Customers hate it when they need to deal with a lot of advertisements while shopping. Make sure that your platform does not allow too many advertisements from apps, games, or other niches.

c. You also need to consider the reputation that your platform. Check the reviews from its previous customers. As much as possible, choose a platform that can generate good reviews to help increase your reputation as a seller.

d. Is the platform SEO friendly? SEO means Search Engine Optimization. For example, if I were a customer looking for "Sunday Dresses" on Google, the SEO support from the platform the generate traffic into your site and your merchandise. Looking for Sunday dresses alone can generate about ten to twenty pages in Google. You need to make sure that your platform can put you at the top of the list.

e. Of course, you will also have financial obligations to consider. When it comes to eCommerce platforms, there will also be costs to take into account. Usually, the more famous a site is, the more expensive its costs are. Surely the reason why is the amount of traffic that it generates for its established sellers.

4. Build your online store. If you do not want to maximize e-commerce platforms, you can also consider building your own online store. Or better yet, to save money, you can use social networking sites such as Facebook and Instagram. But just like any other platform, establishing your name as a seller is not a walk in the park. There are also factors to consider. For example, if you were to use Facebook as a platform for sending, you must create an attractive business page. It takes a lot of promoting and advertising to generate views and endorsements towards your page. Which is why you need to make your own brand – something eye-catching, and something that can entice a customer to open up your page.

5. You can also use your messenger as a customer service channel where you can chat with your potential buyers and entertain queries and suggestions. In your platform, you must take into consideration the process of billing and shipping. Are the merchandise paid for upon delivery, or do you allow external payment methods such as PayPal and direct bank transfer?

6. To endorse your merchandise, you can also use other websites such as Twitter, Tumblr, WordPress, and others to generate more traffic into your web page. If you like, you can also pay sites for advertising. This can cause a tremendous effect on the endorsement of your name and merchandise.

7. Offer Effective Customer Service. One of the greatest determinants of a successful business platform is the customer service provided by the management. You must provide a way for your potential customers to easily contact you for questions, concerns, and complaints. You wouldn't want them to post a bad review about your website since it can take a toll on the traffic generated to your merchandise.

8. Pave a way for Easier Purchase. Customers also like it when there is an easy way to purchase goods and products. They don't like it if there are glitches, advertisements, and other unnecessary buttons or pages to get through before check out. Think about the times when you were the buyer. What were your pet peeves when you go through social media platforms to shop? To make your business successful, you need to take into consideration these factors that can dissuade a potential customer from visiting your page.

How to Build a Famous Brand

As we have discussed earlier, establishing a famous name in the market is a big hype for your buy and sell investment. To do that, there are various ways on how you can make yourself famous in the eyes of millions of consumers per day. Do you ever wonder why famous bloggers earn thousands of dollars per day because of their millions of views? Do you ever wonder how they have established their names on the internet and soon spread like wildfire? Before, they were just like you – aspiring, determined, and persevered to make their own brand. But how were they actually able to pull it off? How did they get millions of supporters and fans to watch their videos and read their articles every day?

When we talk about the brand, it refers to the overall perception of people towards you and your products. It is the "name" or "title" that people know about you. Take for instance the singer Eminem. Because of his song entitled, "Rap God", eventually, people started to refer to him as such. He established his name as the Rap God to the public. Hence, generating more views on his talent and gaining more fans by the minute. Of course, the famous singer also had mishaps and shortcomings because of his haters. But people admire him for how he deals with such issues. Sometimes, he writes a song about his hater, and this actually makes the people love him more. He sticks to his title as the Rap God, hence, his reputation precedes him to this day.

If you watch the NBA League, you are familiar with Stephen Curry, Kevin Durant, and Lebron James. Why do you think their names are catchy during matches and competitions? Why do you think their names stick to the minds of the public better than the others? Simply put, they have established their names on the court due to their gameplay. People can take one look at the game and say, "That is how Stephen Curry plays! Look how fast Durant shoots." Or, "Amazing how Lebron can dunk." They have instilled in the people's minds their highest abilities that stood out among the others.

This is the same in establishing a name in the business. It is not merely creating a tag line that says, "I got it all for you." You need to make the people believe that you have something that others cannot fathom. To do this, you need to consider various steps to make your name famous in the market.

1. What is your business really about? Specificity is the key to your brand. Who do you want to help and what do you offer? For example, you want to create your own store that aims to sell hand-me-downs like clothes, shoes, and apparels at a very low price. How are you any different from other stores? Are your designs better? Is your merchandise affordable for students? How high is the quality of your products? Consider many other factors that can stick in the minds of the public.

2. What is your mission? Why do your customers need your merchandise when they can just choose any other store? You can craft a clear message that gives them an idea that your products are high-quality but cheap in price. You can also include an easy checkout and cash on delivery suited for busy people, like single mothers, students, workers, and many more. You can also create your own tagline, catchy, and interesting. Something that everyone can bear in mind like the Nike tagline: Just do It or create a unique logo that can attract potential customers into choosing your products over others.

3. Study the market including your competitors. It is best to research everything you can about your niche and your brand competitors. What don't they have? When you find these loopholes, you can attract people to patronizing your work by compensating the weaknesses of your competitors. For

example, most of your competitors sell various clothing designs for teenagers, and adults. Why not establish a niche that sells baby apparels along with pregnancy suits and accessories. There, you can start establishing your name as a quality seller of goods. And start to expand as time goes by.

4. Consider your Brand Voice. If your target audience is parents, your brand voice must match their preferences. What kind of tone do they want to hear? Do you need to be professional, friendly, authoritative, technical, informal, conversational and many more? Remember to match your voice to the needs and predilections of your target audience. If your target is businessmen and professionals in technology, you can make your tone professional, technical, and promotional. But if you aim to sell to teenagers and young adults, it is important to sound friendly and welcoming to your audience.

5. Make a clear statement. Finally, when you include your statement on your site or page, make sure to make it brief, concise, and catchy. Something that impresses who you are, what you offer, and the need for your services. Avoid using vague and deep words to your audience as not everyone can understand highfalutin words. I am sure you do not want them to search everything in the dictionary just to comprehend.

6. Make your brand personality shine. Once you established the mission, services, and tone of your brand, give it your best to make it stand out to the crowd. If everyone else seems to be so formal, be friendly and casual in your conversations. In that way, your consumers will feel more welcome and assisted in their endeavors. Never cease to integrate your brand. In every activity you do, incorporate your brand name and your mission. This helps generate traffic to your site and

this helps you stand out from your competitors. When they see your passion and commitment to your business, they will surely patronize your merchandise.

Chapter 8

The Iron Condor

"Sometimes your best investments are
the ones you don't make."

Donald Trump

Indeed, there are times when people remain skeptical about various forms of investment. Little do they know the advantages of having such an <u>investment</u> can do wonders to your life. In the previous chapters, we have discussed the various ways to diversify your assets and profits from a mutual fund. In this segment, I would like to discuss how to choose the right investment for you. It is easy to say, "I want to do this because of it easier, and it is my passion." When it is nice to actually follow your dreams, it becomes a different story when you are too busy to take care of it. See, there are many factors to consider when you want to choose an investment, so let us start with a few steps.

First and foremost, it is important to set your goals. Ask yourself where you want to be in the years to come. Do you have short-term goals or long-term goals? You need to learn how to prioritize for your needs as it comes along in the future. For example, in three years' time, your son or daughter is going to college and you need to earn money for their academic needs. In a span of three years, what necessary investment should you do to save enough? Do you have time to invest in mutual funds or in yourself and following your passion? Or do you earn more in a short period of time through buying and sell?

In setting goals, you need to think of your dreams as a motivation that can drive you towards a better life. It should not pose a threat. Your dreams must not intimidate you nor dissuade you from living your life to the fullest. Also, in setting your goals, you need to consider the SMART Concept.

1. Specific. You must be able to clearly define what you need in the future. It helps to take into account the probable expenses or the total amount of money needed for your goals. For example, in 3 years, you are going to need a car to travel to various states in America. To actually accomplish this goal, you are going to need a specific type of car you want and inquire about the price beforehand. Also, if you plan to travel, how much do you think is needed to see multiple places and try new things? Every time you set your goals you must have a target line. Either you stick to the landing point or you strive for more. In my experience, it is always effective to advance higher than your goals in case of emergencies, shortcomings or any form of setback.

2. Measurable. Your goals must also be accountable. The improvements must be seen by the naked eye or it should reflect the number of assets recorded on your part. Aiming for more abstract goals can be very vague and unreliable. It makes a person take his dreams for granted. For example, avoid setting goals such as, "By the year 2025, my expenses will be reduced by 25%." At this time, there is no saying on what the economy would look like in six years. It cannot be measured. Therefore, it makes an unreliable goal. When you encounter a set back during the process of achieving this goal, you are most likely dissuaded to move forward because

you will realize that there is no point in putting an effort into something that has no finality. Instead of setting your goals in that manner, you can rephrase it by saying, "By the year 2025, I will have a total asset of not less than 10,000 dollars." See, that is an accountable statement because it can reflect on your assets in the long run. And as you forego and continue the methods you employ to reach that goal, you can assess your performance and improvements to make room for more development and innovation.

3. Attainable. You also need to make sure that you set your goals in a way that it can be achieved. When you put too many expectations on yourself and your abilities, there is a great tendency to fall out and breakdown. To set your goals properly, you need to know yourself from the inside out. Determine your skills, strengths, and weaknesses and work your way from there. Make sure that the goals you set are realistic goals for yourself to help boost your confidence and motivation to keep moving forward despite any challenges that may come.

4. Apart from that, setting unrealistic and impossible goals can lead to anxiety and depression. You need to remember that no man is perfect. Everyone is bound to fail more than once in their lifetime. So, in setting your goals try not to be a perfectionist. You will only be putting yourself and the people around you in grave terms.

There are times when we stay up late at night thinking about the millions of mistakes we made in our lives. We start to live up to our regrets and failed expectations to feel depressed and anxious. We also have friends who have set their goals way too high to achieve, only to be left frustrated and hopeless in their goals. But think about it? What is the main reason why we set the bars too high in our lives? Is it really because we want to succeed? Is it because of fame?

Or is it because it was how we were raised by our parents? Believe it or not, there are people out there who were trained by their parents to think as perfectly as they could. Because of this thinking, children have been forced to work very hard, to the point of burnout, distress, sometimes suicide. Some people grew up in a society where medals and awards are very important to the family. Without gold hanging down your neck, people will think of you as garbage and useless. Do not live to please people for what they want for you. Live to please yourself.

By reading this segment, I hope you start to believe in what you can do, not what other people "think" you should do with your life. Set the goals which you think are fit for your lifestyle and your talent. Do not pretend to be somebody you are not just to fit in a damaged society. If you are born within a family who have high expectations for you, break that stigma and start living your own life to the fullest. Set goals that make you a better person, something that makes you determined.

The point is ladies and gentlemen, do not be too hard on yourself when you set your goals. Give yourself room to be human. And us humans are bound to make mistakes from time to time. But these mistakes push us to grow and develop. Everything does not have to be perfect. Your efforts just have to be 100% of what you can give and not what you perceive you can give.

5. Relevant. Next, to be a responsible business owner, it helps to create goals that mean something in your life. Can you imagine yourself making goals that do not matter in the future? If you have such, I don't think you will ever put enough effort to move forward with your goals. This is the reason why you need to choose a goal that makes an impact on your life. It could be for your own retirement, education of your children, luxuries and renovations, and any other goal that could improve your life in the future. When people set

goals that do not pose any significance in their life, there is a greater tendency to give up the second things become difficult. The reason behind giving up is the lack of motivation. Without this, a person is not inclined to employ other characteristics such as self-discipline, confidence, passion, and commitment.

6. Time-Bound. Lastly, you need to set the timeframe of your goals. It is not enough to say "someday" or "later in time." You should be precise in giving yourself a deadline. Ask yourself what you need, why you need it, and when do you need it. These factors will help you determine the actions you are willing to take to achieve the goals in a matter of time. Without a deadline, you are prone to procrastination and idleness. You will not be able to accomplish anything as long as you do not stick to a schedule.

"An investor without investment objectives is like a traveler without a destination."

Anonymous

The next thing to do is to write all these things down on a piece of paper, preferably a journal, and keep it until your due date. When you write your aspirations, it is important to be specific as much as you can. What kind of car do you want? What kind of house do you intend to build? What school will your children go to? Experts have proven that whenever a person writes his thoughts and emotions, his focus is magnified towards his innermost dreams. In the future, that parcel of paper will serve as a motivation to keep moving forward despite the many trials in life. Whenever you feel down, incompetent, and when your life is falling apart, look at the paper once again and let it be a beacon towards your success.

Talk to your friends and family about it. To gain support and to boost your self-esteem, share your goals with your loved ones and talk about it. In this way, you can learn various things from your elders. At the same time, they can help you assess whether your goals are achievable or not. You can also tell them the necessary steps you intend to employ to accomplish your goals. Your friends and family may have some insights they would want to share to make your plans better and more effective. When you share your goals and aspirations to your family and friends, you will start to feel good and confident towards tackling consequences and making huge decisions in your life. You know that they will always be there to assist you and pull you back up when you fail.

To determine which investments to consider, you need to ask yourself about your resources as a business owner. How much do you have and how long can you invest? Do you have enough capital to finance yourself and create your own business out of your talents? Or do you want to have a more liquid form of investment such as buy and sell to ensure the inward cash flow for financing purposes? Assessing how many assets you are willing to invest, you determine what kind of products or services to offer to the public. It will start to fall into place because it helps you narrow down the choices into something affordable yet safe way to diversify your assets.

It is also important to consider how hands-on you want to be. If you have a job or if you intend to become a fulltime mom, what investment is suitable for you. Remember that 80% of your results come from 20% of your efforts. Even when people say that business should be earning money without any effort at all, it should not be the case for you if you want to be successful in your venture. There is no such thing as easy money. In order to achieve your goals, you need to put your 100% into your chosen line of work or investment.

Chapter 9

The Road to Motivation

When I was younger, I longed to be a successful person when I grew up. I wanted to start my own business preferably something that includes building my own style of apparel. Because of this, I invested my time in gathering as much information as I could from movies, social networking sites, and websites on how I could produce the capital needed to create my own brand. For many years, I have been concocting an image in my head of the specific apparels I would like to sell in my store one day. Of course, I was deciding whether to make my store chic for girls and women. But there was also a part of me who would like to fill my store with various designs of men's apparel.

As a teenager, I shared my beliefs and aspirations with my friends and family. But most of the time, they would mock me and say, "You do not even have the marketing skills. How can you become a successful businessman?" In the beginning, it pained me to think that I never really was good at expressing myself. During class recitations, I did not speak much simply because I did not know how. I had the idea in my mind but I couldn't bring out the words to actually say anything. Because of this, I was dissuaded from following my dreams to become a successful businessman. When my mother asked me what course to take in college, I really wanted to enroll in Business Administration but because of my lack of confidence, I decided to take another venture instead. During my years in college, I felt so unhappy and unsatisfied on what my life was heading towards. I did not want this course. I just took it because I felt stupid and unworthy of taking a business class. I was demotivated most of the time. I even neglected to go to school because I thought it was not worth it. Luckily, I was able to surpass my challenges and graduate from college. My professors were asking me where would I go from there. But there was still one dream that I intended to follow. I just did not have enough guts to actually pursue it.

One time, I was asked by the guidance counselor to report at the Guidance Office. I thought it was to claim my Good Moral Character Record, but to my surprise, the guidance counselor talked to me about one of my essays which I wrote in my last year of college. So, I opened up to her about my real dreams and aspirations. I was also able to share the disappointments I had because of the constant bullying I took from my friends. At that moment, she convinced me to pursue my dream despite another form of bachelor's degree. She told me one thing that changed my mindset about myself, "You are enough. Do not listen to the people around who claim that you will not be amazing in your endeavor. Every person is special in their own way. And that dream of yours is what makes you so special. The joke is on them. You know why? Because they never had a dream as persistent as yours. They just let the winds take them to where they should be. But you are different because you aim to take your destiny to your own hands." To this day, these words ring in my head like some form of wisdom that I am eager to share to the rest of the world. Since that day, I worked hard to gain capital. It took me years and thousands of failures but I learned from each and every one of it. Now, I own a very successful shop in America. I dare to say it was a difficult journey. But it was worth it. In the following segment, I would like to share some of the things that helped me get through the challenges as an aspiring investor and businessman.

1. Surround yourself with positive people. It is best to have a few supportive friends and family members to help you get through the hardest times. Lord knows, during my venture towards having a successful business, there were more downs than ups. I was so close to giving up. I was so close to surrendering on my dreams. But in your journey, the will come across many different people. A few of those will become your close friends, some you might even consider as your family. Look at where people can support you and accept your decisions no matter how crazy or risky it looks. Choose people who frankly tell their opinions because they care about your ventures as much as you do. Do not settle for people who will try to change you because the people who are meant to be with you are those who can accept you for who you are. Never mind the naysayers. They only exist to bring you down. Instead of focusing on the negative, push yourself to focus on the good things and stick with it.

2. Stick to your mantra. When I was younger, my mantra was always, "I think, therefore I am." I had my references from Rene Descartes, the founder of the Cartesian Plane. Whenever I feel nervous about a decision or when I feel scared of making another move, I close my eyes for a moment and remind myself of who I am supposed to be. There is beauty in believing in your mantra. It reminds you of how strong you are as a person. It motivates you to strive harder. And it pushes you to come back bolder. Whatever your mantra or your motto is, keep it by heart and never lose sight of it.

3. Think two steps ahead of time. When you constitute your plan for the business it is best to think of collateral strategies just in case your plan A fails. It helps to think two or more steps ahead. Ask yourself what potential setback and

shortcomings might come your way and think of a solution ahead of time. It is very effective to be prepared for every situation in your business. Practice the art of being cunning and wise in making your decisions because it can do wonders towards the success of your business.

4. You are the captain of your own ship. Most people believe that business is a mere gamble and it is just a game of chance. Ladies and gents, this is a big myth. Although there is truth in it because of the risks you need to face in investment, you are the only person who can control the rise and fall of your business. If you put your efforts to minimize the risks and maximize the results, then you have nothing to worry about. But if you plan to take your investment for granted, then you better think twice about moving forward towards your investment.

5. As a future investor in a business owner, it is best to think big and small. Do not disregard situations just because it seems unworthy or irrelevant to your venture. Remember, you will not succeed in bigger actions if you cannot decide on smaller ones. No matter how small a situation is, give it you're all to strategize because it serves as a training ground for harder trials towards further ventures in investment.

6. Remind yourself of your goals. Sometimes it helps to make a visual aid from your goals. You can print it and put it on your wall as a daily reminder of your goals. It also helps if you print out motivational quotations and scatter it all over your work station to have something to think about whenever you feel down or hopeless.

7. Acknowledge that people make mistakes but you need to learn from it. As I have been reiterating over and over again, nobody is perfect but you must be willing to own up to your

mistakes. Do not let your mistakes be a demotivation to your dreams. Instead, take it as a stepping stone for the development of your strategic planning, decision-making, and problem-solving skills.

8. Take care of yourself. Did you know that one of the worst reasons why people become demotivated from their dreams is their restlessness? This is the reason why you need to have sufficient sleep, maintain a healthy diet, and follow a regular exercise routine. These three factors can help you boost your immune system to be strong enough to face a new day. Apart from that, experts have found out that sleep is essential to help your brain and body revitalize after a long day. It helps you reorganize your thoughts in such a way that it would feel refreshed when you wake up in the morning. Sleep is a very important commodity. Whenever you have the chance to rest, do so. Do not deprive yourself of the goodness of sleep because you will need every energy you can harness to become effective in your line of work.

9. Furthermore, it is also important to maintain a balanced diet and avoid junk foods. Nutritionists have found out that junk foods and oily foods can make you feel sluggish. Therefore, you are more prone to procrastination and stagnation leaving you nonproductive for the day. Instead of letting yourself divulge into harmful foods, it is best to exchange your diet with fruits and vegetables that can help you hype your energy at its fullest.

10. Experts have also studied the effects of exercise to the body and they found that facilitates the release of a hormone called the endorphins or the "feel-good" hormone. Whenever you feel down, these hormones are responsible for making you feel better. It is essential to hype a bad mood and to reverberate good vibes all throughout the day. This is the

reason why doctors recommend a regular exercise in the morning to kick start your day making yourself ready for the challenges you are yet to face.

11. Unwind. To help your body recover from the beatings of life's trials, go on a getaway trip with your friends and family. All work and no play causes a fatal breakdown. It helps to relax and rejuvenate once in a while. Call friends for breakfast, lunch, or dinner. Ask someone to join you for coffee from time to time. In this manner, you can help release the tension and the pressure stored within your system to be ready to take more.

12. Avoid comparing yourself to other successful and unsuccessful entrepreneurs. Never think, "What if I end up just like him?" or "I have been in this business for ten years, how come he got more successful than I am?" You need to remember that life is not a race. There is no reason to be frustrated if you come last from the group as long as you made it. There are factors why it happened that way. Maybe it was their resources or connections. But whatever you do, never compare your status to anyone else because it will either bring you down and demotivate you, or it can pump up your ego and make you greedy. And let me tell you, greed is the cause of your untimely downfall. Nothing good ever happens when a person turns greedy or impulsive in making his decisions.

Conclusion

Investing mutual funds is never an easy investment. It takes effort, time, and perseverance to become successful. But do not be dissuaded easily. Even if you are not an expert in business or investment, I believe that every person is resilient in nature and there will always be room for learning and growth. No matter how much you think that you are incompetent and useless, I want you to believe otherwise. Remember that no man is an island. The reason why you will need a fund manager and a fund advisor is to have guidance in every decision you make. You are lucky to have your friends and family who are willing to support your endeavors and will accept you no matter how many times you fail.

What matters in mutual funds investment is your commitment to work hard for profit. You must be willing to learn tactics and strategies you can employ for future reference. It is not enough to say, "I know enough." or "I do not need to know anything else." The market is an ever-changing environment. Trends change, taxes change, preferences change, and strategies can change over time. You need to adjust to these changes to really succeed in mutual funds investment. Change is the only permanent thing, so they say. And as a responsible entrepreneur, it is your duty to stay curious and inquisitive about any idea that comes your way. It doesn't hurt to keep a journal of every learning come across every day in your life. In fact, it can help you reflect on your strategies in decision-making tactics to make your plans better as an investor.

We have also discussed how you can manage the risk in your investment. For this, I want you to remember never to lose hope in yourself and your investment. I hope you stick to your passion and vision to become successful in the future. Remind yourself of your dreams over and over again until it wipes out every hint of doubt and self-loathing within your heart.

Once you have garnered a profit, it is best to diversify into different classes of assets such as proprietorship and buy and sell. For these endeavors, you need to keep a consistent mindset towards the success of your goals. Remember that 80% of your results come from 20% of your efforts. Imagine what would happen if you put 100% out of 100% of who you are in your line of work. A dare says, after reading this book, I will be with you in the next conferences, seminars, and workshops to come. Who knows? After 10 years you might be the one giving the lecture on how to be successful in mutual funds investment and in the diversification of assets. Think big. Never let other people limit your dreams. By this time in the next five years, I might be seeing your face on the cover of a magazine, sharing your experiences as an aspiring businessman or a businesswoman.

You can just imagine it from here. You are now in your sixties, and you're sitting on the front porch of your very own home by the beach. Your children are calling your name and say breakfast is ready. You smile at the wind, feeling thankful for all experiences you had to get here. In those moments, you may shed a tear as you remember the hardships and trials you had to get through to reach success. But when you look at where you are now, you can say that every drop of sweat, blood, and tears were totally worth it.

CPSIA information can be obtained
at www.ICGtesting.com
Printed in the USA
LVHW042201170120
644013LV00010B/710